Antique Needlework Tools

The Story of
Antique Needlework Tools

Bridget McConnel

4880 Lower Valley Road, Atglen, PA 19310 USA

Library of Congress Cataloging-in-Publication Data

McConnel, Bridget.
The story of antique needlework tools / Bridget McConnel.
p. cm.
Includes bibliographical references and index.
ISBN: 0-7643-0710-X (hardcover)
1. Needlework--Equipment and supplies--History. 2. Needlework--Equipment and supplies--
Collectors and collecting. I. Title.
TT845.M37   1999
746.4'028'4--dc21   98-51410
CIP

Note: the conversion rate used for the values in this book was $1.60 to the pound sterling.

Designed by Bonnie M. Hensley
Type set in Shelley Allegro BT/Goudy OISt BT

ISBN: 0-7643-0710-X
Printed in China
1 2 3 4

Published by Schiffer Publishing Ltd.
4880 Lower Valley Road
Atglen, PA 19310
Phone: (610) 593-1777; Fax: (610) 593-2002
E-mail: Schifferbk@aol.com
Please visit our web site catalog at **www.schifferbooks.com**

In Europe, Schiffer books are distributed by Bushwood Books
6 Marksbury Avenue Kew Gardens
Surrey TW9 4JF England
Phone: 44 (0)181 392-8585; Fax: 44 (0)181 392-9876
E-mail: Bushwd@aol.com

This book may be purchased from the publisher.
Include $3.95 for shipping. Please try your bookstore first.
We are interested in hearing from authors with book ideas on related subjects.
You may write for a free catalog.

Contents

Acknowledgments

With sincere thanks to the following people who have supplied information and photographs, especially those who allowed me to publish items from their private collections. Without their fine contributions, this book would not have been possible.

Betty Aardewerk
Sonia Cordell
Helen Eastgate
Judy Pollitt
Pat Rich
Gay Ann Rogers
Nerylla Taunton
Hedley Wood
Pam Morris
Molly Pearce
Ruth Mann
Wendie Ritchie
B.W.G. Wttewall
Dr. and Mrs. L.B. Forward
David Morgan

Museums, organizations, and shops:

The British Museum
The Victoria and Albert Museum

The Petrie Collection at University College Museum and the University of Manchester
The Royal Maritime Museum, Greenwich
City Museum, Western Park, Sheffield
Sotheby's of Bond St.
Phillips Auctioneers, Knowle, West Midlands
The Peterborough Museum, Peterborough
S.J. Phillips Ltd. Antique Silver & Fine Jewels
Pillows of Bond St.
John Jaffa Antiques
Arca Antiques, Grays Mkt. London
Times Past Antiques, Portobello Road
Betty Aardewerk & Sons, Holland
Lawrence Gould Enamels and Fine Objects, Portobello Road

Friends and family who have given their unfailing support, endless patience, and technical expertise:

Annie Elkins
Josephine and Kenneth Firth
Geoffrey Whitehead
Sheila Pusinelli
Andrea Dekker
Lydia Townsend

Compared with other antiques, little has been written about needlework tools. They have long been taken for granted as part of the fabric of every household, hardly deserving serious attention. Now that position is changing, and more information is being sought. There are not many fields of collecting that reside in the female domain; up until recently, textiles, dolls, and fans have been the only ones that easily came to mind. Now needlework tools, such as fitted sewing boxes, thimbles, châtelaines, and étuis, have become important enough to warrant specialized sales in all major auction houses. Now is a good time, therefore, to seek out as much information as possible, so that you may venture with confidence into this delightful field.

One of the most valuable ways of gaining knowledge is by studying private collections, whenever the owners have been kind enough to make them available. Many of these contain articles that have not been photographed before, partly because until recently needlework tools have not been in the forefront of antiques. The benefit of looking at a collection that has grown through time is that some articles will have long since disappeared from the marketplace. Due to the generosity of several collectors, this book will demonstrate that advantage.

Many collectors find their initial response to antique sewing tools, with all their variety and charm, is one of affection. To open up an old sewing box that has been in a family for generations and take out its very personal contents is to gain unique access to certain aspects of that family's history. Such boxes were often used as secret stores, and one finds letters from loved ones, invitations to balls, shopping lists, and diaries hidden among the sewing things.

One such box (shown on pages 158-160 in the chapter on Collections) revealed many such mementos amongst the more usual implements. There were letters dated 1820 from a ship's officer, complete with descriptions and tiny water color sketches of each place that he visited. A bird's feather, a pressed flower, a blade of exotic grass, all identified in the letters, had been preserved by the recipient in the folds of a needle-book, tied with faded blue silk ribbon. There was a book of fashion designs for women's bonnets, tiny baby's shoes, and a pin cushion with a message for someone's birthday. There were round boxes the size of your little finger-nail, containing beads as small as grains of sand, and half-repaired net purses housing old shopping lists. These hidden delights, alongside the tools of elegant craftsmanship, are to many the very stuff of collecting, as they help to illustrate the stories of past private lives.

Earliest Historical References

The current state of our knowledge indicates that sewing tools go back to at least c. 30,000 BC. The earliest example of sewn work is to be found on the clothing of a Cro-Magnon man found preserved in the ice of Vladimir, Russia; his fur boots and cap were decorated with ivory beads made from animal tusks. Bone needles dating from c. 15,000 BC have been taken from Neolithic settlements found in caves in France. Palm-pushers, an early type of thimble device, along with needles made out of porcupine quills, bone, or wood have been found in Neolithic sites in Europe, Africa, and China. By 5000 BC, a very successful weaving and sewing industry had developed in the valley of the Nile in Egypt. There are many examples, now catalogued and on view by appointment in the Petrie collection, of fine cutting blades, flax thread reels, needles, and bodkins excavated from the Egyptian tombs at Naqada from the pre-dynastic period (before 3150 BC).

Palm-pusher, an early type of thimble device.

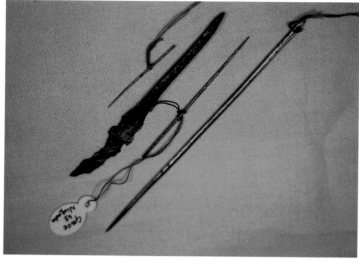

Needles and a cutter from the pre-dynastic period (before 3,000 BC), excavated from the tombs of Gizeh and Rifeh. *Courtesy of the Petrie Collection.*

Hedgehog design on a bracelet. This design could have been mistaken for a device to push needles, had the design been reversed.

Expandable rings with raised hedgehog design. *Courtesy of the Petrie Collection.*

China

Just as the Nile valley was famous for its flax production, so China was famous for its silk. We know that it was the Chinese who first produced silk from the larvae of the Bombyx moth. The mulberry trees, on which the larvae feed, were not introduced into Spain, Italy, and France until the sixth century AD. The earliest pure silk, some of it embroidered, was Chinese, but by the sixteenth century the Middle and Near East and later Italy and France were becoming equally famous for their fine exports. The problem is that virtually no early textiles remain to us that pre-date the second half of the sixteenth century, with the exception of some embroidered textiles made for the Church. The latter survived due to their infrequent use and careful handling. The quality of the general sewing and embroidery on these is superb.

A Short History of Needlework

The earliest pieces of delicate stitching that have survived date from c. 5000 BC and were found in ancient Egyptian tombs. The linen cloth, made from flax, was of excellent quality and would have been sewn with fine needles. Bodkins (used for holing or threading when working thicker materials) of wood, bone, copper, silver, bronze, and gold have also been recovered. Products of the Persian and Babylonian civilizations in existence c. 3000 BC have also survived. The Babylonians are believed to have invented gold-work around that time, using spun gold thread, a technique which the Egyptians were later to develop further.

Fragments of Egyptian tapestry embroidered with fine thread on a linen cloth (now in the Egyptian Museum, Cairo) date from c. 1550 BC and employ some of the Egyptians' favorite design motifs. These include the lotus flower, egg and dart designs, rushes, and the leaves and blossom of the honeysuckle. Expensive gold thread was used for the most prestigious pieces of work, whereas gilded catgut was employed as a less expensive alternative, for instance in the work decorating Solomon's temple.

By the first century AD, the art of embroidery was so sophisticated that Virgil was moved to describe it as "painting with a needle." From the first to the fourth centuries, Rome produced much embroidery done in purple wool on linen. Indigo was the most expensive dye and purple therefore became the color associated with the Emperors and the aristocracy. The most common motifs in Roman embroidery were human figures, animals, and foliage, particularly trailing vines. By the end of the fifth century, Egypt was exporting embroidery that incorporated Christian symbols and scenes from the Gospels. Byzantium, too, was famed for the needlework it produced during this period.

By the tenth century, Sicily had succeeded Byzantium as a leading center of art and was exporting the Arabic designs so typical of the pre-Norman period in that region. In England, the art of embroidery flowered between 1250 and

1350, carried out by men, by whom the Broderers' Guild was established. This gave rise to a body of work known as the *Opus Anglicanum.* The Syon Cope in the British Museum is a fine example of the standards of the time. A proportion of the most beautiful English embroidery of this period was designed by monks, who otherwise specialized in illuminating manuscripts.[1] The actual sewing was done mainly by women. In addition to monks, the designers of embroideries were professional men who traveled the country to carry out commissions.

Italian embroidery flourished in the fourteenth century, particularly in Florence. Francesco Squarcione, founder of the Paduan school of painting, was especially renowned for his work in embroidery design—it was common, principally in Italy, for tapestry and embroidery designs ("cartoons") to be produced by painters during this period.

Perhaps the most attractive shaded gold-work ever produced emerged from the rich courts of the Dukes of Burgundy, based in Flanders in the fifteenth century. Known as *or nue* (naked gold), the tradition of rich embroidery work expanded during the following two centuries and influenced fashions at all the European courts. Precious stones and brightly colored intricate designs of flowers and foliage, often using black silk thread on linen, were widely employed on both clothes and domestic items, such as cross-stitch samplers and boxes covered with padded stump-work.

Petit point, the finest form of needle-point, was widespread in seventeenth century France, and by the eighteenth century, enormous quantities of needlework were being made throughout Europe, including wall hangings, clothes, samplers, and silk pictures (landscapes among them). The focus of English embroidery had also become domestic and courtly rather than ecclesiastical, following the Reformation and the Dissolution of the Monasteries. In fact, the declining production and the disappearance of many of the skills associated with the sewing of ecclesiastical embroidery were only finally arrested in nineteenth century England when the resurgence of the High Church and the consequent demand for greater ecclesiastical ornamentation promoted the revival of decorative embroidery on vestments, pew seats, and other church furnishings.

This trend towards decorative embroidery was regrettably reversed again at the end of the nineteenth century with the invention of the sewing machine, both domestic and commercial versions, which initiated another decline in embroidery standards. The long-taught skills of domestic needlework, exemplified above all by the delicate and often touching samplers of young girls, radically deteriorated.

A brighter note to finish on is today's renewed interest in sewing in its social context. Perhaps the lack of interaction provoked by television and by working from home on a computer has stimulated the growth in popularity of sewing groups. There are quilting circles in the United States and Canada, for example, and lace-making and embroidery groups in Europe and Asia. The lace bobbins, the tatting shuttle, the needle, and the thimble are valued not only for the instrumental nature of their work, but also for their role in encouraging the binding together of communities and the exchange of information between them.

Chapter One

Medieval Europe

In Medieval Europe the hours that women worked were long and hard. Households were often greatly extended, consisting of parents, children, kinsmen, and various servants and laborers. All these people relied on the home economy of the housewife. Although it is wrong to assume that there were no specialized trades such as baking and brewing to help out, there was precious little spare time. Most women carried their spindles with them throughout the day so that they could spin thread which would later be sold for turning into cloth. An idle moment would have been undreamed of. Everything in a household had to be sewn, repaired, or darned—from the family's clothes, to household linen, wall hangings, and floor coverings. Sewing tools were a vital part of domestic life.

Outside the home, women had to settle for the lower paid jobs: they were denied entry into the trade guilds, which meant that they were denied "the freedom" to set up a business. A man could serve his apprenticeship as a tailor, enter the guild, and then—having completed his training—apply for the freedom to set up his business in the town. Women could not be apprenticed, so they had no formal training. Consequently, women who worked in the cloth industry were usually engaged in low status positions, such as spinners, washers, pattern cutters, and sewers. A woman, however skilled in any form of sewing, could only secure herself a wage that was barely subsistence level. The only exceptions were widows of guild members who could continue in business[1] under their husbands' names.

As a typical example of women working in textile and sewing related trades, take Emma Taillor, also called Hosiere,

who made stockings for a living in Exeter in 1377. Emma was able to run her own business, but because she had not received skilled training and lacked the privileges of "the freedom," she could not hope to advance to a prominent position within her chosen industry, as was the case for many women. Furthermore, Emma could not borrow the capital through the guilds to fund a business or seek assistance during difficult times. Indeed the situation was such that women could not receive training or recognition, as they were forbidden membership into trade institutions. This meant that female fields of endeavor, such as sewing, and later lacemaking and dressmaking, were forced into low status positions.

This situation did not change for centuries. Even in late Victorian Britain, the social historian Henry Mayhew[2] describes the work of the seamstress as "so poorly regarded, that it warranted the lowest wages, thereby often forcing the hapless girl into prostitution, especially if she had any dependants." The contradiction has always been that tailoring was regarded as skilled and well paid, because it had its own formal institutions and apprenticeship system, whereas dressmaking was not.

To get an idea of sewing tools that were used in general domestic sewing in Medieval Europe, the British Museum is your best source. The Medieval scissors and thimbles on pages 11-18 are part of a collection of antiquities lent by David Morgan, one of the few collections to incorporate many early working tools.

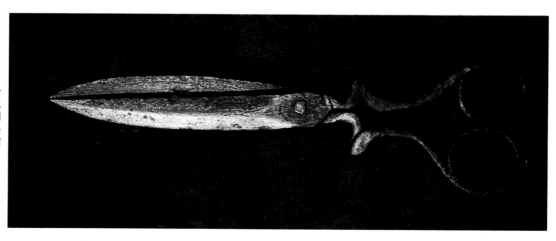

Steel scissors, probably fourteenth to fifteenth century, English, excavated in a field outside London. Unidentifiable owing to lack of records. *David Morgan Collection.*

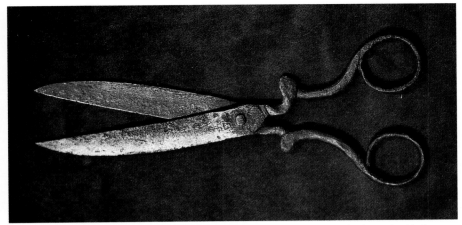

Reverse view of the same scissors on page 10. Note the maker's mark where the blades join. *David Morgan Collection.*

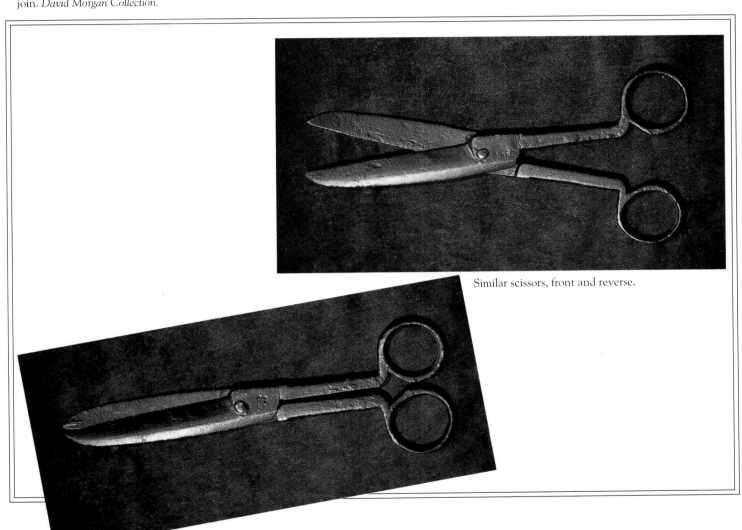

Similar scissors, front and reverse.

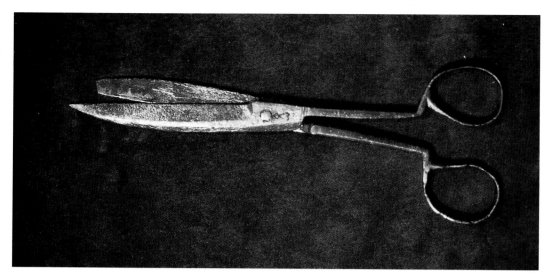

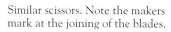
Similar scissors. Note the makers mark at the joining of the blades.

Again, similar scissors.

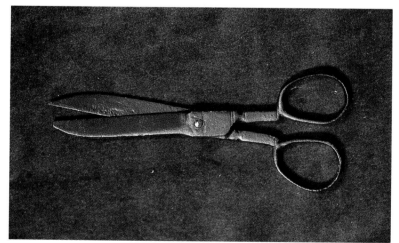

These scissors are from David Morgan's private collection of antique working tools and small antiquities.

A mixed group of early excavated thimbles. Top, from left: Levantine, probably fourteenth to fifteenth century; slim Hispano-Moresque with Arabic lettering inscription. Bottom, from left: thirteenth to fourteenth century open topped tailor's thimble; fourteenth to fifteenth century European thimble; extremely rare early example of a pusher in the manner of a sailor palm, possibly fifteenth century, excavated in England; another example of an open topped thimble; European, fourteenth to fifteenth century with a decorative quatre-foil top. Allow over $160/£100 each.

Another mixed group of excavated thimbles. Top, from left: tailor's ring; Hispano-Moresque. Bottom, from left: fourteenth to fifteenth century European, pierced top; fifteenth century European; Hispano-Moresque.

13

Two European thimbles
excavated in Spain.

A fifteenth century brass
European thimble.

A fabulous gold Hispano-
Moresque thimble. Approximately $4,800/£3,000.

When you look at groups of artifacts excavated from Medieval sites, you may be struck by the large quantities of pins. These were made from fine drawn brass wire, with a round and often decorated head attached. The decoration can vary from a plain sphere, to one pierced all over. Some pins even have animal heads, or swans on the top.[3] The larger pins look more like prickers, but they were pins, in the manner of a brooch pin fastening two pieces of a garment together. The reason why you will see such large quantities is that many of the garments worn were secured by pins rather than other fastenings. At first glance the humble pin might seem to lack variety, but not so! With the gradual evolution of pins through Venetian glass, precious stones, and silver to gold, they could form a novel collection on their own. They are not expensive, and can still be found.

Chapter Two

Perhaps the most important event in a girl's life, and one that had to be planned from childhood, was marriage and the accompanying provision of a dowry. In sixteenth century France and England, even girls from well-to-do families were sent to other noble families to learn the necessary accomplishments. They were paid for this work, and the money was then put aside for their dowry. One of the skills taught was needlework; others included singing, dancing, basic literacy, and numeracy.

Amongst the poor, a young girl on a smallholding would glean the wool from the hedgerows, spin it into thread, and sell it for cloth. Quilts were made and stuffed, simple garments sewn. A girl without a dowry faced spinsterhood or, in countries such as Spain, Italy and Portugal, life in a convent. A girl of twelve was considered an adult, and her best chance of securing a dowry was to leave home and work in another household, often not returning until she was twenty-five.[1] That was how long it took for a girl to set herself up for the future and provide her portion of the marriage dowry, which included all her household linen, quilts, hangings, and clothes, as well as cooking, sewing, and spinning tools.

For sewing tool collectors, the sixteenth century signifies the introduction of the Nuremberg thimble. These fine, brass thimbles were made in the city of Nuremberg in Germany, using a process called annealing. Briefly, this meant hammering out the shape from sheet metal, then heating it at intervals in a furnace, to keep the brass pliable. These thimbles are still to be found. If there is a maker's mark, it will be found at the start of the dimpling. Increasingly, those with fine decoration will become more costly.[2] If you are lucky enough to find a silver Nuremberg, the price could be over $500 (£312). Brass pins and bodkins can also still be found. A bodkin is a large needle without a sharp point but with a big eye, used mainly for threading cord or ribbon. Blades and scissors do turn up from time to time, so look at the point where the scissors join, as that is where you may find a maker's mark.

Two sixteenth century tailor's sewing rings.
Courtesy of the British Museum.

A Nuremberg thimble.
Approximately $320/£200.

Only a few early sewing tools are available to us now, with the exception of pins and thimbles. Silver examples of any tools are very rare. Until the end of the fifteenth century, German silver mines had been the main source of silver in Europe and proximity had therefore led German craftsmen to acquire exceptional silversmithing skills. However, these mines were almost exhausted by the beginning of the sixteenth century. This may be one of the reasons for the popularity of brass Nuremberg thimbles, and for the rarity of any remaining to us in silver. Europe increasingly looked for its supplies to the new silver mines being discovered by the Spanish in South and Central America. This greater diversity of sources led silver to become more widely available than ever before, enabling other craftsmen all over Europe to develop their own traditions in silver-working and its associated arts. If you ever see an early silver thimble, it may bear an inscription, which will help with identification.

Engraved Lettering

When you are trying to date an early sewing tool, it may be useful to note the manner of any engraved lettering. The earliest black letter (double outline lettering) engraving appeared at the end of the fourteenth century, and from that point on inscriptions are plentiful down to the Renaissance.[3] Capital letters were not used as this would spoil the design. In the fifteenth century it became usual to have a capital letter at the beginning of any inscriptions. Black letter inscriptions continued in use until the first quarter of the sixteenth century, but by the end of it were competing with Roman capitals, when any inscription at all was executed in crude Roman capitals, being practically scratched on. This was partly to avoid being accused of Popery, a culture known for its elegant lettering and use of Latin inscriptions.

A sixteenth century thimble with a pierced top. Note the gilded border with black letter engraving. According to Charles Oman in *English Engraved Silver*, black lettering or double line lettering was used from the last quarter of the fourteenth century to the first quarter of the sixteenth.

Of course, it would be a lucky collector who found any sewing tools from the sixteenth century, the most likely items being thimbles, pins, and bodkins. Scissors or various forms of cutting blades might also be found, and those imported from the continent could be decorated with engraved Renaissance designs. Italian collectors are known to have fine early scissors collections, and there is a book on antique scissors published in Italy that has good photos, but hardly any text. Possibly Germany and the Low Countries might have more early silver pieces, owing to their silver mine productions. Due to accumulated dowries, some early fine tools remain in private collections in Europe. Others might have been given to the local convent. Convent thimbles are understood to have an old tradition attached to them, as they were the only personal possession a nun was allowed to keep. It is rumored that girls sometimes slipped a ring of value over their thimble, where it looked like part of the border and would go undetected.

Netting began in the sixteenth century, but the netting sets seen in most antique shops today would be the eighteenth and nineteenth century versions. Netting is a simple craft, and the tools required are a netting needle and a gauge for the hole required. The object of the craft is to make nets and netting for numerous purposes: fine net for the hair, medium for purses and small articles, and coarse for curtains and bed hangings. Mary, Queen of Scots netted "furniture for a bed of network" while she was imprisoned in 1567; sadly it was never finished. The early nineteenth century sets are often enclosed in ivory tubes, inside which are various gauges for different sized holes. Fine nets were often used as background for white embroidery, then made into a charming cap for the hair.

We get much of our information regarding domestic sewing from important country estates where there has been a continuity of family records. However, records from big cities tend to give us a broader picture of sewing as a commercial enterprise. By 1583, there were large numbers of foreigners living and working in and around London, this being mainly due to the religious wars in Europe which continued intermittently between 1562 and 1629. Persecution of the Protestants in France caused the exodus of many Huguenots from Paris. These highly skilled craftsmen settled mainly in Spitalfields, in the east end of London, and in Norwich and Exeter, alongside the Flemish weavers who had come from the Low Countries. Their main skills lay in the innovative weaving techniques they used for fine silks and half silks.

A group of brass spoons and two gold mounted knives. Although not sewing tools, these objects, supplied by David Morgan, help to show the style of the period.

A selection of brass thimbles excavated in Britain.

Left to right: brass thimbles probably made in Nuremberg; a pewter needle case with handles either side, on both ends; a pin with a decorative head; three cloak fastenings, the top middle one showing the flat Tudor Rose.

Carved stone spinning whirls. A stick was placed in the center and the stone "wheel" spun the wool out.

Pilgrims' badges and fasteners. Again, not sewing tools but a helpful aide to style identification.

The Dutch immigrants were given their own church, in Austin Friars, around which many of the other immigrant workers gathered. By the end of the century, trades people tended to live and work in specific areas; goldsmiths and silversmiths, for example, were mainly located in Cheapside and Lombard Street. It would be nearly impossible to find gold or silver sewing tools from this period, as so much was lost or melted down to use as a form of currency. This is the reason for the enormous price of $28,000 (£18,000) fetched at a Phillips auction in 1992 for a late sixteenth century gold thimble set with stones. Not only was it a very important thimble, it was rated alongside rare and important Renaissance jewels, of which few remain. The stones themselves are a mixture of sapphires and rubies with paste replacements added over the years. As with all antiques, the precious nature of materials used is always of secondary importance to age, rarity, and excellence of design and workmanship.

Elizabethan thimble referenced in the text as having fetched $28,800/ £18,000 as an example of fine Renaissance workmanship.

Chapter Three

The Seventeenth Century

By the seventeenth century, the dowry demanded to secure an aristocratic husband was so substantial that in most cases a father could only provide enough for one daughter. Often the amount was as high as twelve times the father's yearly income. The manner of providing a dowry by working either with her needle, or in a general domestic way, was not open to aristocratic girls. These unmarried daughters were obliged to live as spinsters at home or enter a convent. This century saw an enormous increase in the number of unmarried aristocratic women owing to the escalation in bride-price. For example, as many as one third of the female Scottish aristocracy remained single. When we look at the considerable amount of embroidery undertaken during the century, this may be one of the reasons!

The seventeenth century saw a great increase in domestic embroidery and the use of textiles in wealthy houses. Wall hangings, designed to bring warmth and color, featured allegorical subjects in the Elizabethan tradition, such as the Virtues and their Contraries. Different hangings were required for each season and when someone of importance died, the house was entirely hung and covered with black.[1] Upholstered furniture was the new fashion, partly because better built houses and more efficient chimneys made comfort easier to achieve. Raised work and general embroidery embellished cushions, samplers, pictures, mirror surrounds, bed hangings, draught screens, nightcaps and slippers all were in constant demand. With greater domestic stability, more attention was given to luxury and fashion.

At the dawn of the century, most households must have looked rather sparse and lacking in personal character and intimacy: porcelain had not yet been imported, pottery was very basic, and furniture and wall paneling were in dark English oak. There was a dearth of decorative ornament to give warmth and life to a room. Towards the middle of the century, furniture became lighter as oak gave way to walnut, and the fashionable new tall backed chairs had brightly colored upholstery and embroidered squab cushion seats. Typical furniture of the time would be padded and upholstered, secured by rows of metal studs, the most recognizable design being variations of strap work used on textiles, silver utensils, and sewing tools, particularly sewing compendiums (see Chapter Four).

The single most important event to shape the way that people's houses looked in the sphere of the domestic decorative arts was the formation of the East India Company in 1601. All the sumptuous textiles, the delicate and luminous porcelain, the softly glowing lacquer, the light and airy chintzes, tumbled out from the warehouses of India, China, and Japan into the somewhat lackluster English households. Filigree silver from India became a vogue. Sewing items such as thimble cases in highly decorative filigree, enhanced with tiny flowers and leaves, were bought by the rich. Of course, all this new exotic luxury delighted the affluent who preferred everything imported rather than English manufactured goods. This resulted in great poverty and hardship amongst workers, particularly the silk weavers in Spitalfields, who then had to endure unwanted competition from a further influx of Huguenot weavers from France in 1685. When you next look at early tape-measures, needle cases, and sewing boxes, notice the silk used inside. It would have come from Spitalfields or Norwich, gossamer fine, in subtle and glowing colors.

Engraving entitled "Threading the Needle." Note the hanging scissors, the pin cushion, and needle.

Two seventeenth century silver thimbles.
Courtesy of the British Museum.

A seventeenth
century silver bodkin.
$288/£180.

A rosewood lucet. Because the wood was
decorative rather than functional, there is
a split where the first hole was placed, due
to strain. A contemporary repair has been
carried out by placing silver-plate over the
first hole; a second hole had to be drilled in
the handle as a result. Luckily the
silversmith who carried out this repair left
his initials D.H. on the plate. This could
stand for David Hennel, working at the
beginning of the eighteenth century, in
1730. Approximately $320/£200.

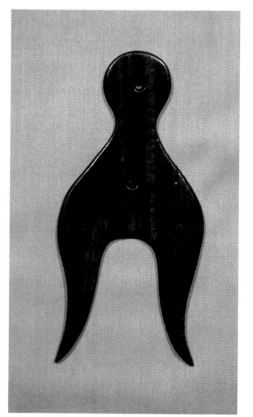

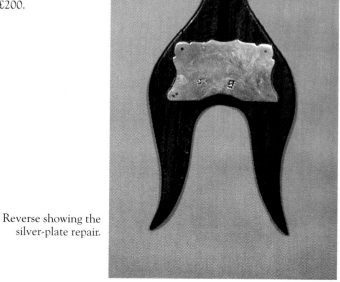

Reverse showing the
silver-plate repair.

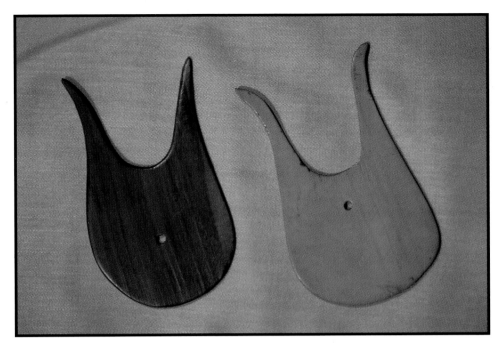

Examples of two different wood lucets, probably eighteenth or even early nineteenth century. As the design has changed so little, it is difficult to be accurate. They have been included here to give the reader an idea of construction. Approximately $96/£60.

Lace

Clothes have always been important as an outward display of class and wealth. In the seventeenth century this applied even more to male attire. Certain materials were worn at court, such as embroidered silks, satins, and lace. Costume details in seventeenth century portraits are a good source for seeing how textiles, embroidery, and particularly lace were used. In both the seventeenth and eighteenth centuries, men spent more money on lace than women. Court records show that William of Orange spent $4,000 (£2,500) for several items in 1695, and that is a paltry sum when compared with prices paid at the French court. Despite some faltering steps in the sixteenth century, needlepoint and bobbin or bone (pillow) lace did not fully emerge until the seventeenth century. Then Italy, France, and Flanders became the great lace-making countries.

Flemish pottery figure from Bruges of a lace maker with her lace making pillow, c. 1880.

In France, early lace was known as *passement dentele*. A rough translation of *passement* is trimmings, hence the use of *passementerie* describing the trimmed decoration surrounding a stump-work picture, or sewing casket. The word *dentele* means toothed or indented; later the word *passement* was dropped and in France lace is known as *dentelle*. If you look in old inventories, you may come across the words "laced" or "laced up," which does not always mean fastened together by laces or cords. An early form of covering seams, or "lacing up" sewn garments, was achieved by laying a *passement* or braid of lace over the seam. Orris, which was lace woven with gold or silver thread, was often used for this purpose, especially on court dress. These costly braids and trimmings were sold by lace-men, or *passementiers*. The workers making the braids were mostly women working from home..

Lace tokens were invented in the mid-seventeenth century by an enterprising lace dealer in Olney.[2] There was often a shortage of change, so James Brierly produced a token to give instead. It shows "James Brierly B.I.M" on one side with "of Olney 1658" on the reverse. There were probably many more minted, but records are scarce. There is mention of two seventeenth century tokens issued at St. Neots, Huntingdonshire, showing two lacemakers on either side of a pillow and "The Overseers of Their Halfe Penny" on the reverse. These items are rare, but they turn up occasionally in old sewing boxes, button boxes, or lace bobbin boxes. More familiar lace tokens are from the eighteenth century, when a token size was approximately 1 1/4 inches (33 mm).

Guipure is one of the most famous styles of needle-point lace. It originally came from Venice and subsequently became very popular in France. It is extremely fine, made using only a needle, possibly a pricker, and a spool knave for the thread. A typical Guipure design would be of flowers built up in an amazingly three-dimensional way, giving a rich encrusted appearance. Lace and fine crochet work are indistinguishable to the inexperienced. Some of the most famous crochet is Irish, which has the appearance of coarse lace, often with charming little flowers dotted about on collars or doilies. Here a fine crochet hook would be used, and, depending on the thickness of the thread, interchangeable heads might be screwed onto the handle. As a collector, you might look for crochet sets—some are cylinder shaped with the handle in the central hole and various hooks in the surrounding holes. If some of the hooks are missing, you can buy some inexpensive ones and replace them. In the nineteenth century, many of these sets were made in Mauchlin ware; since crochet work tended to be done in humbler surroundings, local materials were used.

There are many different lace-making techniques in Ireland alone. Carrickmacross, for example, is famous for its delicate cut out muslin shapes, often of flowers, appliquéd onto fine net.[3] The net would have originally been made with a netting set or been commercially acquired. Limerick tambour lace, using a tambour hook to carry out the delicate chain-stitching, is exquisite. Tambour hooks can be made of simple bone, with a steel "butterfly" screw at the side to keep the steel head in place, or they can be made of precious materials. Because crochet work was often done on the move, hooks were usually made of cheaper materials, but tambour work had to be done seated at a frame. Tambour hooks were made from ivory, cornelian, gold, ivory inlaid with silver, and tortoiseshell, sometimes with the handle and hooks fitted into a shagreen case.

A sample of Irish lace.

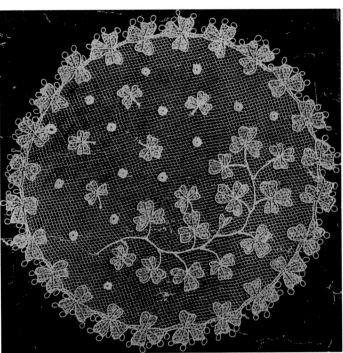

Another sample of Irish lace.

Catalog page showing border design of
Carrickmacross Guipure.

23

Bobbins

Amongst lace specialists, needle-point is considered the finest. Bobbin lace is less prestigious because it is coarser. However, bobbins themselves are very sought after. For collectors of tools, the most commonly collected within the lace-making field would be bone bobbins, the main difference between British and foreign bobbins being the British addition of beads, properly called spangles. When you know more about bobbins, you will be able to recognize different makers from their particular areas. These include Bobbin Brown of Cranfield (1793-1872), whose spiral lettering is bold and clear, and Joseph, David, and Robert Haskins of Bedfordshire. The latter made a great variety of magnificently decorative bobbins, with gold leaf, loose rings, wire, and even inlaid turquoise, from the middle of the eighteenth century to c.1855. Each maker had his own shape and style.

The glass "spangles" at the end of the bobbins were often made *gratis*, from sweepings off the floor of the local glass blowers. They are therefore sometimes called "end of day" beads. The oldest beads are square, with marks like tiny waffles on each side from being fashioned while still hot between tiny wood pats, like butter pats. The men were allowed to turn the droplets of glass into beads by piercing them with a hot needle, ready for their girlfriends' bobbins. The items that you find at the ends of bobbins are often curious mixtures. You may find charms, coins, medals, and buttons. If you want to repair a spangle end, use some fuse wire and collect old beads to thread on the wire.

A selection of British lace makers' bobbins with spangles at the end. Bone: approximately $24-48/£15-30 each. Bone bobbins with names on: $48/£30 each. Bone bobbins with mottoes on: up to $96/£60 each, depending on the rarity. At the bottom of the picture there is a silver arrow-shaped knitting needle holder with a chain for suspension, c. 1850. $128/£80.

Another selection of
wooden bobbins priced
from $7-16/£4-10 each.

Example of a Tunbridge ware
bobbin holder box with the
tumbling cubes design; various
bone bobbins, decorated with
tiny beads, shown on either
side. At the back are three
different examples of lace.
Approximately $128/£80.

England was the only country to use beads, due to a royal tax on imported fine thread imposed during the reign of George II in 1748. The tax made the imported thread prohibitively expensive. Thereafter, lacemakers had to weigh the coarser English thread down, to keep it flat on the pillow. Glass beads were attached to the bobbin ends for weight. This meant that English lace could not achieve the fineness of its overseas rivals.

Bobbins were engraved with names, mottoes, souvenirs of hangings, weddings, and funerals. These were often carved from the local ham bones. A typical motto might be "I love the boys," or you might find a name and a date if you are lucky. Bobbin boxes are attractive. They are typically about 8 inches (20 cm) long, made with wire hinges, and in a local wood, although the more expensive ones might be made in Tunbridge ware. When you are next traveling through France, watch for local lace museums, complete with tools. They are numerous and of an excellent standard.

More Seventeenth Century Tools

Lacemaker's lamps are also a delight to collect, although not strictly a tool. They are sometimes known as "flashes."

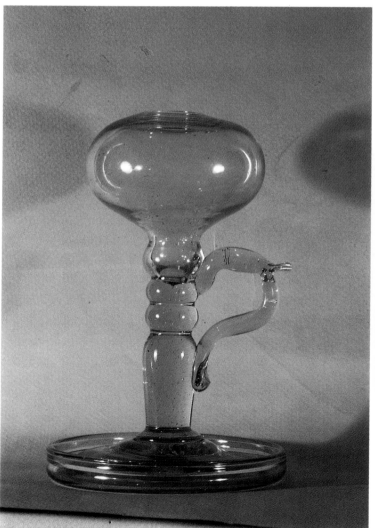

They are always made of glass, filled with water, and used to magnify and reflect the light from a candle placed behind the lamp onto the piece of work. The shapes vary; some have handles, some a decorative stem, some are miniatures, perhaps for traveling. A pretty display can be made in the corner of a room, with a spinning wheel and a lacemaker's pillow, complete with colorful bobbins. Adjoining, one can put a small table covered in a lace cloth with a lamp, a wood bobbin box, lace prickers, and a variety of tambour and crochet hooks. Lace itself can be framed, creating a beautiful wall decoration. Displaying tools, by re-creating a sympathetic space, can lend grace and individuality to a room. Lace-making countries have a richer store of lamps, tambour and crochet hooks, tatting and knotting shuttles.

Ordinary folk in London wore wool and adapted fashions to their working needs. When you look at the heavy textiles worn by the majority, you can understand why everyday tools had to be stronger and coarser. Repairing thick wool breeches would require a strong brass thimble, a thicker needle and heavy iron scissors, whereas embroidery would require fine needles protected against rust by a silver case, sharp pointed light scissors so as not to rip the silk, and a dainty thimble to avoid snagging the stitches. In France, there has always been a tradition of fine tools made of iron, sometimes damascened, pierced, or decorated with gold inlay. The best collection of fine iron sewing tools is in the museum of Henri Le Secq des Tournelles in the Museum of Rouen. If you find a steel case with the scissors missing, do not worry, buy it if it is handsome. The same may be said of a thimble case, as they are collected in their own right and these early tools are very scarce.

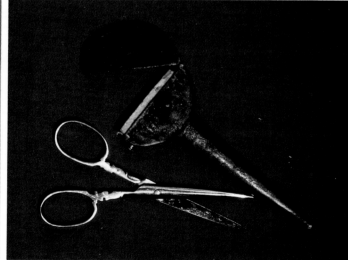

Late seventeenth or early eighteenth century scissors and case. The scissors are made in fine steel and the case is in black shagreen (fish skin).

A lace maker's lamp. I am indebted to Dr. and Mrs. Leslie Forward for their help in researching the lace and lace bobbin section. $480/£300.

It is still worth looking in the Paris *Marché aux Puces* for early iron tools. Drizzling cases, used for unpicking and for cutting metal thread, are often found without the two side unpicking tools or the central scissors, but again they are so rare that they should be purchased. There is an elegant silver drizzling set listed as seventeenth century in the Museum of London. The side tools would have been used to unpick the gold and silver trimmings and the scissors to cut the thread. There is a story that many an officer in dress uniform would leave the dinner party table with his fancy epaulettes in tatters, due to his neighbor's skillfully applied drizzling set, while with flattering insistence she demanded "You must tell me about your last campaign." Perhaps a miniature spinning set, to wind on the precious thread, had been smuggled in under her cloak.

All but very simple garments were made by professional tailors, with materials chosen or brought in by their clients. There were no retail shops as we know them today, just one room workshops in the poorer areas, and out workers who were mainly women and children. Tailoring was not expensive; in 1608 the cost of making a young man's suit was £2. Tailor's shears are sometimes found, but it is extremely rare to find a seventeenth century tailor's thimble (that is, an open ended thimble ring, enabling greater pressure to be exerted from the side). Ornamentation could be enormously costly: an embroidered perfumed leather waistcoat and panels, executed with silver and gold thread, cost £45. Fashion accessories, such as ribbons, lace hats, and gloves, as well as elegant sewing tools could be found in smart shopping areas such as The Strand. The poorer people would buy from street markets and the traveling peddler, whose wares always included scissors, needles, and thimbles made in iron and brass.

After the elegance and luxury of the court of Charles I, its halo effect spreading down over the aristocracy, came the shock of the Commonwealth with its doctrines of Puritan austerity. The Civil War in England had a marked effect on all the arts and crafts, including the making of sewing tools. Whereas silver had been widely used before the Civil War—albeit often gilded—it suffered the same fate as other metals and was frequently melted down. This was to provide material for weapons, armor, and helmets or to raise money. Most pieces that survived are remarkable for their sloppy workmanship, clumsy construction, and relatively plain appearance. There was no time to waste making pretty things when England was being torn apart by a bitter conflict. In the seventeenth century, religious wars raged over most of Europe.

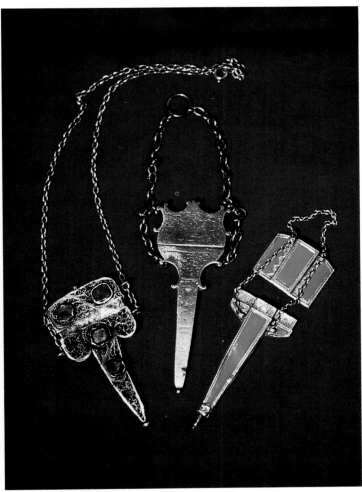

Two scissors cases and one drizzling case. From left: silver filigree scissors case embellished with glass stones; engraved silver scissors case; blue enamel and silver drizzling case without the tools. The scissors would have fitted into the center, with a stiletto or unpicker and a little knife, to cut the thread, in the slots on either side. $640/ £400 for each.

Silver châtelaine comprising a combination thimble and needle case, a pin-ball, and a scissors case. The chains are joined to a plain ring worn threaded onto a belt. Note the rather perfunctory engraving.

In Holland, however, Protestantism in no way cramped decorative styles. Holland's decisive victory over its Spanish enemies brought independence by the middle of the century, as well as peace and financial prosperity. It is fair to say that the seventeenth century was the high point in Dutch creative productivity. Relative economic stability prevailed again after the war with England and the Civil War, fostering further technological advances. If you are able to find Dutch tools from the middle of the seventeenth century, they will be decidedly more decorative and better made than their English counterparts. Certainly Dutch thimbles were finer and more innovative.

In France, during the reign of Louis XIV, there was tremendous interest in anything Chinese and the style of *Chinoiserie* became a craze that swept through the aristocracy. This was due to an ambassadorial visit from China to the French court at Versailles. The Chinese wanted iron ore, and in return they had come to trade their luxury goods. They sent the French court wild with such a display of wonderful lacquer, porcelain, ivory carving, fans, silks, and fantastic embroidery that from then on, everything fashionable had to be Chinese. They stage-managed the event with brilliance: these extravagantly dressed figures, with their parasols and pagodas, long fingernails, and black moustaches, must have looked like visitors from another planet. The courtiers were agog with astonishment, as they breathed in the perfumes and incense, marveled at the jade carvings, and ran about chasing the little dogs that the Chinese court officials released from their sleeves. This is why, if you look at engravings on metal sewing tools of the period (for instance scissors cases), you may see charming Chinese faces and figures depicted.

Reverse of the scissors case at lower left.

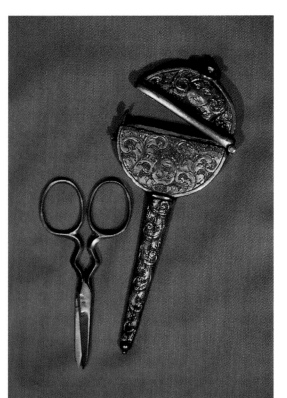

Gilded metal scissors case, possibly on a copper alloy base. The scissors inside are also gilded metal but they are not contemporary, probably eighteenth century. Note the engraved Chinese faces, probably made after the Chinese ambassadorial visit to the French court. Also note the join down the back of the scissors case, the hinges, and clip, all made in a typical seventeenth century manner. $624/£390.

A combined thimble and needle case in silver, engraved with a typical strapwork design. Note the similar finial to the Chinese figures scissors case. A small round blob at the end was a favorite seventeenth century finishing device. The handles either side would have been for suspension chains.

One way of telling seventeenth from eighteenth century engraving is by the difference in the strokes. Fine sweeping strokes were not achieved until the eighteenth century. This was due to an improved engravers tool, the Burin, not to a lack of skill, for one has only to look to the engraving on seventeenth century Dutch glass for proof of that skill. The Burin was made from strong, tempered steel in the eighteenth century. This enabled the engraver to apply more pressure, allowing a greater fluidity of movement. Previously, the engraver had to be cautious when pressure was applied, as the tool sometimes broke. Only short jagged marks were therefore possible, with the result that earlier designs appear more cramped.

After the Restoration

During the eleven years of the Commonwealth (1649-1660), production and consumption were considerably curtailed and no woman would dare admit to owning a frivolous châtelaine or thimble. One of the most lasting reminders of the Puritan influence is to be found in the wealth of religious mottoes, mostly of a depressing nature, found on many sewing items. Mottoes such as "live to die" are found on the borders of silver thimbles or embroidered on pinballs—enough to put you off doing anything in case you are taken heavenwards at any moment!

With the Restoration of Charles II, general prosperity increased, and people could enjoy their homes in safety. Brightly colored stump-work was one of the fashionable styles of embroidery, carrying on the tradition of padding and embroidered upholstery used on furniture. However, it was mainly used to create pictures and cover sewing boxes, looking-glass mounts, and caskets. Stump-work was originally called raised work. The designs, which were ready printed on a background, were taken from a jumble of Old Testament stories, then combined with scattered flowers and oversized insects. One often sees faces and hands in a flesh pink, an effect which was achieved by wooden or parchment molds of faces or hands. These came in a kit, covered with flesh-colored silk.

Samuel Pepys, an upwardly mobile civil servant but not a wealthy one, writes about frequently visiting his tailor to have his clothes remade in the current fashion. Pepys also writes about the popularity of oriental imports: "To Temple Bar to an Indian shop to buy a gown and a sash which cost me 26 shillings" (*Diary*, 1667). Poorer Londoners purchased their clothes in the markets of Houndsditch and Long Lane, most of the stock there being acquired legally, although there was a flourishing trade in stolen clothes: "Stolen out of the parsonage at Much Brackstead, a new mantua gown and petticoat" (*London Gazette*, 1690).

As the century closed, rich and poor alike were relieved to see the end of the religious wars that had torn Europe apart. Now designs found on tools celebrated the secular and the personal, such as initials entwined with hearts and cherubs. Home life could be enjoyed once more, and fashionable houses blossomed under the influence of a king who brought an appreciation of beauty learnt from his years in exile. The stage was set, and the audience ready, for the debut of some of the most beautiful sewing tools ever made.

A typical later seventeenth century silver thimble with scratched lettering around the border reading "Do not loose me." $720/£450.

A thimble designed by Joh. Theo de Bry.
Courtesy of the British Museum.

Scissors case in silver also designed by
Joh. Theo de Bry. Both this and the
thimble shown above are from the late
sixteenth century and illustrate neo-
classical Renaissance motifs. *Courtesy of
the British Museum.*

Chapter Four

The Eighteenth Century

If you ask most sewing tool collectors to choose their favorite period, it would be the eighteenth century. This was when the House of Hanover ruled Britain, having been invited over from Germany because Queen Anne had left no heir. All the Hanoverian monarchs were called George (except the last one, William), which was convenient and gave rise to the term "Georgian era." Because the Georges preferred spending most of their time in Germany, Parliament became stronger than the king, as is the case with absentee landlords. Many reforms were undertaken in working practices, which eventually led to that burst of technological energy and invention in the early nineteenth century, commonly known as the Industrial Revolution.

At the beginning of the eighteenth century most work was done by hand, but owing to the invention of machines powered by water and steam, this gradually began to change. As the century progressed, we can see a growing use of technology, so that by the end of the century, Britain had become the most important manufacturing country in the world. Although so much has already been written about the elegance of the period, it is difficult to think of it other than as a golden age of beauty, balance, and ingenious invention. It could be said that the century belongs to the French with regard to their influence in the field of the decorative arts, and to the English in relation to furniture. Most of the sewing tools that remain to us from this period are instantly recognizable for their practicality, refinement of execution, and simple delicacy.

For example, we have only to look at the combining of natural materials, such as the iridescent mother-of-pearl with gilt metal mounts, in the manufacture of sewing tool sets. It is such a seductive combination, especially carried out in the neo-classical style of the 1790s. These alluring items often become the high point of any collection. There appears to be a harmonious balance between machine precision and individual design with hand-finished ornamentation. This balance was typical of The Age of Enlightenment, when Art and Science were expected to walk hand in hand for the benefit of mankind. With sewing tools, that aim was achieved.

An agate étui set with semi-precious stones. *Courtesy of S. J. Phillips Ltd., Antique Silver and Jewelry of New Bond Street, London.*

Enamel

Enamel étuis are amongst the most personal and charming sewing tools made during the Georgian era. They came predominantly from Battersea in London and an area in the Midlands known as South Staffordshire. This was because the body under the enamel was made in copper, obtained from the Ecton Hill Copper Mine in Staffordshire.[1] When buying enamels, it is important to look for as good a condition as possible. There will always be some hair cracks, but they must not detract from the painted surface. If you ever need to have an article restored, the hardest part to re-do is the lettering; for example, if there is a motto. The original lettering would not have been done freehand and it is very difficult to achieve the original mechanical look. Today, if you see freehand letters within a more precisely rendered motto, chances are the article has been restored.

As a rule of thumb, the more colors used, and the brighter and truer those colors are, the better quality the object. This is because each color has had to be fired separately, and during firing the colors alter, depending on small changes in temperature. It is a high risk enterprise, as too many firings can ruin the colors; therefore, only a master would risk it. A glaze was applied after firing, as experience showed that a glaze inhibited potential damage from scratching. English glaze is softer than the glass-like finish on foreign enameling, which is one way to tell a continental piece. The mounts were made in ormolu or pinchbeck, then gilded and polished. On the whole, English enamels, painted with pastoral scenes, have a soft, natural appearance reminiscent of an informal English garden. One reason why antiques in general have such an aesthetic appeal is the softness brought about by the gentle integration of surfaces over time. This is why any restoration must be attempted with caution.

If you want to specialize in collecting enamel tools, you should be aware that the firm of Samson of Paris copied eighteenth century enamels in the early 1900s. The best way to tell if an article is a copy is by the quality of the painting. The original eighteenth century examples were finely detailed and the color gradations subtle, giving depth and life. The Samson copies, although at first glance colorful and seemingly in better condition, can look bland, crude, and lifeless next to the real thing. If you look at a Samson étui, the painting will appear stiff, lacking the spontaneous delicacy of the original. If you imagine yourself copying something, you can understand how concentration would cause an inhibiting stiffness to your hand. The originals were probably dashed off, albeit with skill, but with some attention to being cost effective!

The subjects painted on the originals, both in England and abroad, were inspired by French court artists such as Boucher and Fragonard. They featured pastoral idylls, favored by city dwellers who rarely visited the country! It is doubtful if a real shepherdess ever possessed the pretty dresses she was painted in, dallying with her swain. The enamel articles that you can collect now are thimbles, needle

Left: enamel combination needle and thimble case, beautifully hand-painted with exotic birds. $1,280/£800. Right: tortoiseshell and silver piqué bodkin case.

Porcelain, hand-painted thimble case, with ormolu mounts. $560/£350.

cases, bodkin cases, and fitted étuis. These charming étuis, or equipages, are fitted inside with metal tools, such as tweezers, bodkins, a folding knife, folding scissors, and perhaps a tiny ivory leaf notebook and pencil. The ivory leaves of the book could be wiped clean each day. As they were nearly always made to order, few étuis are exactly the same. It is important to buy as complete an example as you can, because the tools are nearly impossible to find separately. In a desperate situation, borrow a tool to copy, then go and plead with a talented silversmith.

A good quality enamel thimble on its own will enhance your collection, but be prepared to spend over $1,280 (£800). Regarding bodkin cases, the bigger ones tend to be misnamed sealing wax holders. Most good auction rooms try to sort out a wax holder from a bodkin case, but smaller auction rooms do not. Ask for the measurements over the phone, or take a bodkin, or very large needle, in your purse and put it inside for size. If it gets lost, it's a wax holder. Needle cases are always smaller, often cylindrical in shape and not usually too pricey. Another item to look out for is a combination thimble and needle-holder, which in good condition will be over $1,600 (£1000). You will not find one containing the original thimble, as that would have been a separate item. All these charming enamel items are expensive, but they add great charm and color to a collection.

An enamel egg containing gilt metal tools, hand-painted picture of a shepherd and shepherdess in pastoral setting on exterior. $2,400/£1,500.

An enamel bodkin case with cupids. $720/£450.

Enamel thimble. $960/£600.

Eighteenth century enamel étui, opened.

Enamel bodkin case. $640/£400.

Shuttles

Knotting shuttles, especially in enamel, are some of the most beautiful eighteenth century tools to collect, but we are talking over $1,600 (£1000) each. Knotting was the aristocratic pastime of making little knots into an edging resembling lace. The knots varied in size, depending on the thickness of the thread. The edging could be used on a great variety of garments or hangings, to finish off or trim. The most ravishing display of shuttles in enamel, gold, silver, piqué, and mother-of-pearl, can be seen at The Wallace Collection in Manchester Square, London. Although what is produced by a knotting shuttle could be considered pedestrian, the shuttle itself has its own glamour, with a large flat surface ideal for decoration. The French name for knotting shuttles is *navettes*, due to their resemblance to little boats. The ends of the shuttles are always open.

Tatting, although it carries out a similar function, appears to be the poor relation, as the shuttles are smaller. Tatting shuttles can be found in a delightful variety of materials, carved and inlaid, and the bonus is that they cost much less. Tatting really came into its own in the 1850s-1860s, so will be discussed in more detail in the following chapters. The late eighteenth and early nineteenth century tatting shuttles have open ends whereas, as a general rule, mid-nineteenth century tatting shuttles have closed ends.

Two knotting shuttles, one in mother-of-pearl, the other in silver-gilt filigree. Approximately $640/£400 each. The smaller two shuttles (in mother-of-pearl and tortoiseshell) are for tatting,. Approximately $128/£80 each.

Mother-of-pearl engraved knotting shuttle. $640/£400.

Piqué work on a tortoiseshell knotting shuttle.

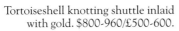

Tortoiseshell knotting shuttle inlaid with gold. $800-960/£500-600.

A knotting shuttle in gold and enamel with neo-classical motifs, English, c. 1780. *Courtesy of S. J. Phillips Ltd., Antique Silver and Jewelry of New Bond Street, London.*

A smaller knotting shuttle in amethyst and white enamel on gold with a central medallion of plaited hair, English c. 1780. *Courtesy of S. J. Phillips Ltd., Antique Silver and Jewelry of New Bond Street, London.*

Working Women, their Crafts, and Tools

During the eighteenth century, women's working patterns and home industries changed considerably. In a real rural landscape, the shepherdess was more likely to be a farmer's wife. In order to increase the family income, she could make lace, make buttons out of horn, and knit. During times of war and revolution, women have always seized the chance to move into jobs and positions of power previously denied them. Although Britain did not experience a revolution as the French did, that major turning point in history had its effect on women in Britain, especially those who worked. Seeing the example of their French sisters, their consciousness was raised as to what could be achieved. By the 1800s there was a tremendous upsurge in women working in welfare and as teachers;[2] at the poorer end of the scale, the farmer's wife could still be a lacemaker, a commercial spinner with her jenny, or make gloves, hats and shoes from her farm.

Changing Conditions

Manchester and Glasgow were becoming important manufacturing centers, challenging the supremacy of Indian imports such as cotton. The East India Company still flourished; indeed all things Indian were the rage, especially the light and colorful chintzes. Porcelain from China continued to be intensely popular and still very expensive. A general merging and incorporation of all designs from India and China led to an English appropriation of the style known as *Chinoiserie*. The most extravagant example of *Chinoiserie* is the Prince Regent's Palace in Brighton, later called the Pavilion. Everything in the way of furniture, porcelain, lacquered sewing boxes, and textiles in the Pavilion follows that style. Instantly recognizable with its domes and minarets, the Pavilion is featured on many sewing tools of the period, such as thimbles, pin cushions, tape-measures, and clamps. The craft of lacquering, also known as japanning, became popular for sewing boxes; these were fitted out with ivory tools and sold to the growing markets of the affluent.

Because of their past history in textiles and the vast fortunes accumulated thereby, you will find that Glasgow and Manchester have some marvelous collections to view. In Glasgow, be sure to visit the Burrel Collection: the textiles, samplers, and few sewing tools are outstanding and it has one of the most beautiful thimble cases in the shape of a bird that you could imagine. In Manchester, there are many fine collections of Victorian paintings, but the Town Hall has a wonderful collection of ceramics, pictures, wall hangings, and general Victoriana of high quality.

Old Sheffield plate was invented in 1743 in Sheffield as a cheap substitute for silver. The industry continued until the mid-nineteenth century when it was superseded by electroplating, a technique that used less silver and required less skill on the part of the workmen.[3] Silver and copper are metals of a similar hardness, and when a thin sheet of silver is fused onto an ingot of copper, the two metals act as one and can be rolled out to any desired thickness. The copper ingot could have a silver surface on one or both sides, depending on the article to be made, but where the back or inside of an item did not show, it was usually left as copper, or, occasionally, tin.[4] As all old Sheffield plate items had to be made from a plated sheet, it should be possible, on pieces like needle cases or étuis, to see the seam where they have been soldered together. With electroplating, areas where the items have been joined together are disguised by the final thin layer of silver. Old Sheffield plate items which show signs of wear sometimes have areas of copper visible, but this is not infallible, because electroplating is also frequently done on copper.

As a point of interest to collectors whose other passion might be textiles, after the First World War (1914-1918) a famous fabric enterprise was started in Sheffield. Annie Binden Carter wanted to provide work for badly disabled soldiers, who otherwise faced a life dependent on charity. Following the late nineteenth century ideal of setting up a Utopian community, she opened a workshop and provided houses for the men and their families, calling the community Eden Village. There she started designing, making, and marketing painted fabrics. The painted designs were based on avant-garde motifs, inspired by Bakst for the Ballets Russes, and abstract subjects drawn from the modern painters of the period, such as Picasso and Mondrian. The fabrics became famous and very fashionable at the beginning of the Art-Deco period. Unfortunately, the thriving factory was closed down and all production ceased at the start of World War II.

Silver thimbles with steel tops, made by Hester Bateman (her initials HB are found sideways round the border). Approximately $800/£500.

Dutch silver thimble case and pin holder. $400/£250.

A Dutch silver thimble with typical border of hunting dogs.

Pinchbeck

To return to the eighteenth century, pinchbeck was a similar invention to Sheffield plate in that it provided a cheap alternative to gold. Queries often arise over the definition of pinchbeck, used to make so many sewing items, especially châtelaines. Here we have a further example of eighteenth century inventiveness. Strictly speaking, the name pinchbeck should only be used on articles made by the inventor Christopher Pinchbeck. The alloy he invented was of copper and zinc, which, gilded and polished, was a perfect substitute for gold. Mr. Pinchbeck was a clock- and watch-maker of Fleet Street and alongside his watches he sold châtelaines, snuff boxes, étuis, frames, buckles, and all manner of "toys." Indeed, he referred to himself as a "toyman," which at the time meant a maker of fashionable gifts, not items for children to play with. A similar alloy was used in France and Germany called Similor or Goldshine, first produced by Renty of Lille c.1729, later improved upon by Leblanc of Paris. As Pinchbeck died in 1732, he was possibly ahead of his French rivals; indeed articles bought in Paris are sometimes marked "pinsbeck."

The most attractive pinchbeck sewing tool is possibly the complete châtelaine, which opens its large central pendant to disclose folding scissors, a knife, a bodkin-cum-earspoon, a pencil, and tiny ivory notebook. Of course the contents vary enormously, as most of these items were custom-made. On either side of the central pendant, you might have a container for a thimble, which, if you were exceedingly lucky, might be the original one in pinchbeck, as well as a container for breath sweeteners or a pin cushion. Ormolu, a name given to describe a gilded metal, is practically interchangeable with pinchbeck, although it should really only be applied to gilded bronze. Thimbles, needle cases, pin containers, and tape-measures (rare) are all articles that were made out of gilded metal alloys, either pinch-beck or ormolu. They are always of the highest quality both in execution and delicacy of form, again using a good combination of machine precision and handwork. In some cases, the ormolu is inlaid with a hardstone, such as onyx or bloodstone, which can look very decorative.

A five piece châtelaine. Left to right: a thimble holder; needle and bodkin case; tape-measure case; scissors case; and either a second thimble holder, pin cushion, or breath sweetener container. $1,280/£800.

Two small thimble holders on either side of a filled central étui containing scissors, notebook, tweezers, and penknife. $1,440/£900.

Five piece châtelaine, possibly with a sealing-wax
container. $1,120/£700.

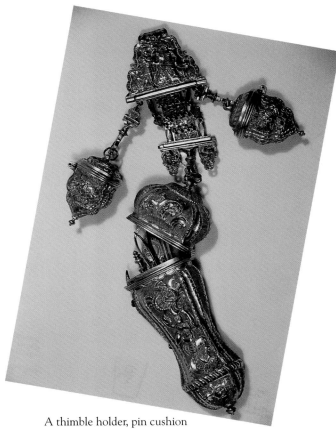

A thimble holder, pin cushion
holder, and central filled étui.
$1,280/£800.

The same, plus original
ormolu thimble which is rare
to find within the châtelaine.
$1,440-1,600/£900-1,000.

Silver Filigree

We associate silver filigree items in sewing with the 1700s and the early 1800s. In fact, filigree was particularly popular in England towards the end of the seventeenth century, following the marriage of Charles II to the Portuguese Catherine of Braganza in 1662. Filigree work originally came from India, and Bombay, which is Portuguese for the Good Bay, was part of her dowry. At first, fairly large caskets came over, but then, owing to their popularity, silversmiths from India arrived and set up workshops. Eventually the technique became incorporated into the manufacture of English everyday objects. Certainly filigree thimbles, bodkin cases, and thimble cases were made in the seventeenth century, but many more remain to us now from the late eighteenth century. Italian silversmiths also excelled in this technique, the largest settlement of Italians being registered as living in Clerkenwell in the 1780s. Amongst many collectors, in fact, the name Clerkenwell work is synonymous with eighteenth century filigree.

Construction details can help serve as a guide to dating pieces of filigree. The 1680 pieces have heavier "skeletons" than their later counterparts, the main ribs being slightly thicker and made from 1mm square section wire. This is filled in with the typical tiny wire scrolls, made from two fine wires twisted together. The scrolls or circles only go round approximately once. In England, the hinges on, for example, a seventeenth century box or thimble case were always made from plain silver. The whole box has a slightly firmer, heavier, and more symmetrical look than an eighteenth century piece. In contrast, on mid-seventeenth century articles from the continent (for example, Holland), the hinges were made from twisted silver wire, not plain silver. The reason for this was because the general silver gauge was thinner and therefore did not have the weight to solder onto.

In the eighteenth century, the filigree "skeleton" was lighter. The secondary "loops" are often longer and have the same shape as the paisley design, which also originated in India where it symbolized the seed of life. The loops are in turn filled with tiny scrolls or circles, which by now are much tighter, going round three times. This sort of work is typically found on the taller, slimmer thimbles and thimble toys containing scent bottles. The squatter thimbles are either late seventeenth century or early to mid-eighteenth. Their small size makes them harder to date accurately and, not being a fashionable object, they were probably subject to less marked changes. Nineteenth century filigree is often even tighter and thinner in look, with less marked changes between the skeleton and the in-fill wire circles.

In the eighteenth century, you would find tape-measures, needle-books, cylindrical needle cases, scissors cases, shuttles, pin baskets, and châtelaines, all made in filigree. Various combinations were later used in making thimble toys, the most famous being a thimble screwing onto a base containing a miniature scent bottle, as first appeared in the preceding century. The scent bottle can be made of clear or blue glass.

Other variations included thimbles combined with a tape-measure or a pin cushion. Some had a finger guard that screwed onto a base containing a tiny emery cushion, the guard then covered by a thimble; sadly, it is now almost always missing. The bases of these toys often had engraved initials which are thought to have been used to seal letters. Châtelaines in filigree are rare, and should be purchased even if the odd piece is missing. The continental ones tend to have longer chains, and the chains themselves are not always in filigree. Filigree châtelaines should really be regarded as fashion accessories and items of jewelry, as well as sewing tools. They were certainly worn on elegant dresses at social engagements, as is evident in paintings of the period. There is a very fine collection of filigree objects at Chatsworth in Derbyshire, home of the Duke and Duchess of Devonshire.

The Household Seamstress

All the invention and new technology, especially in the textile industry, meant a gradual movement away from hand work towards mechanization. Hand work was used mainly in the areas of trimmings and embroidery. Many of the great houses employed a live-in seamstress, often an unmarried gentlewoman of no private means. In exchange for bed, board, and a small wage she would sew household linen, embroider coifs, caps, slippers, cushions, and hangings. Bed linen was often embroidered in the eighteenth century, when whitework was favored, as it stood up well to wear and washing. Brass thimbles and needle cases, and perhaps a steel waist hanging equipage (later to be called a châtelaine), would be the tools of the seamstress. Some Quaker women were employed thus. A member of a Quaker family told me a little of her history, when she sold her thimble. The thimble was plain silver, following Quaker principles of no frivolous ornamentation, and had a steel top. It was engraved Anne 1792 on the plain band and had the maker's initials, H.E., at the side. At this time, there was still a big gap between the pretty ormolu, pinchbeck, and mother-of-pearl tools made for occasional embroidery and the steel and brass items used by working women.

A seventeenth century trinket box with an inlaid picture of a boar hunt, decorated with glass stones. Note the similarity to the seventeenth century scissors case shown on page 27. *Courtesy of the Duncan Campbell Collection.*

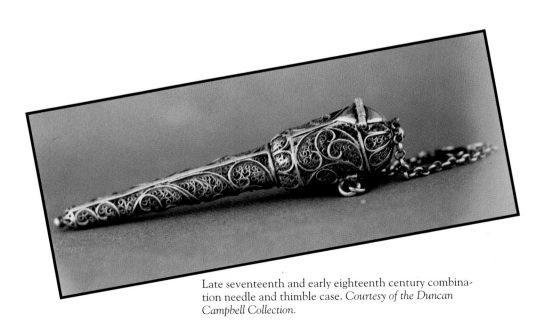

Late seventeenth and early eighteenth century combination needle and thimble case. *Courtesy of the Duncan Campbell Collection.*

Small eighteenth century box which could
have been used for pins. *Courtesy of the
Duncan Campbell Collection.*

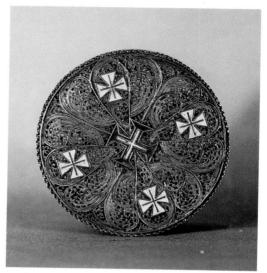

Another small eighteenth century box decorated
with painted porcelain Maltese crosses. Malta
was another famous center for filigree work.
Courtesy of the Duncan Campbell Collection.

Top: a seventeenth century mirror.
The filigree cover slides back to reveal
the mirror which is approximately 4"
across. Bottom: tiny silver filigree
châtelaine with a scissors case,
eighteenth century. *Courtesy of the
Duncan Campbell Collection.*

Detail of typical eighteenth century tops to a needle case and a thimble. *Courtesy of the Duncan Campbell Collection.*

Detail of two additional eighteenth century thimble tops.
Courtesy of the Duncan Campbell Collection.

Needle case, late eighteenth century.
Courtesy of the Duncan Campbell Collection.

Glass scent bottle and filigree container.

Two thimbles and a "toy" containing a scent bottle,
late eighteenth and early nineteenth century.

A tall silver thimble, late
eighteenth century.

A gilt filigree egg-shaped thimble case, lent by Judith Pollitt.

An assortment of items, including a pin box, thimble, needle case, combined thimble and needle case, box, and—on the stand—a miniature bowl for trinkets. *Courtesy of the Duncan Campbell Collection.*

Close-up of the silver-gilt, late seventeenth century trinket box shown in the previous photo. It is decorated with hand-painted porcelain plaques. *Courtesy of the Duncan Campbell Collection.*

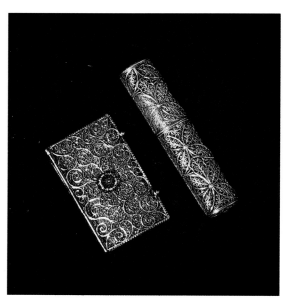

Two needle containers, one in the form of a book and the other cylindrical. *Courtesy of the Duncan Campbell Collection.*

Palais Royal

Palais Royal tools are synonymous with luxury. Delicate, with an ethereal beauty, they are the aristocrats of the sewing items, the complete opposite to the Quaker thimble. The typical material used was mother-of-pearl, fished from the warm depths of the South Seas, then often mounted in Paris with gold or ormolu. These tools sometimes bear small oval plaques in gold with a central enameled flower, usually a pansy. Semi-precious hardstones, such as onyx and agate, were also used in the making of such tools as needle and bodkin cases. The name Palais Royal comes from the Palace of the Duke of Orleans. The Palace was originally built in Paris in 1629 for Cardinal Richelieu and was called Le Palais Cardinal. Later it became the residence of the powerful Duke of Orleans, who renamed it Le Palais Royal. The Duke desperately needed to raise revenue, so he decided to build and rent out shops in the palace grounds. The story goes that the King asked his brother, the Duke of Orleans, to dinner and in front of the court said "I must remember only to invite you on a Sunday, now that you are a shopkeeper!"

The shopkeepers of the Palais Royal enjoyed the patronage of the court and of wealthy, fashionable visitors who wanted to return with delightful souvenirs from Paris. It was said at the time that, owing to the predominance of cafés, boutiques, and ladies of easy virtue ready to offer a more personal souvenir, the area had become an open air brothel! When you next visit Paris, walk down the Rue de Rivoli, eat a marron-glacé in Rumplemeyers, go into the Louvre des Antiquaires, and breathe in the *louche* romance that was once the famous Palais Royal area. Nowadays, Palais Royal is often applied as a generic term for excellence and delicacy of style, and applied to small eighteenth and nineteenth century articles in mother-of-pearl and hardstones, made in Paris.[5]

Tools in mother-of-pearl to look out for are figural needle cases, such as quivers, animals, male or female figures (both very rare), or various cornucopia and flower baskets. The earliest items are probably not mounted in gilt. Try to find the legendary thimbles, mounted with two gold bands and a gold shield or oval pansy set centrally. Hunt for scissors—often with wonderfully carved handles—featuring serpents, swans, even poodles. The finger loops may be cracked, as they are so fragile, but they can be restored carefully. Something less expensive to look for might be stilettos or prickers, and occasionally little mother-of-pearl tapes with gilt beaded sides. The tool sets are sometimes housed in small boxes made in light honey-colored woods. Inside they may have a silk cushion for protection, and embroidered pads on either side to hold the pins, flanked with snowflake mother-of-pearl silk winders. The French court ladies must have looked like alluring mermaids, their mother-of-pearl thimbles flashing to and fro, reflecting the candle-light as they sewed.

For those of you interested in the shell itself, it may be interesting to know the names of the different colors of mother-of-pearl. When you are trying to match pieces in a set, you become aware of the varying dominant shades. There is gold back oyster, also called Goldlip, which has a faint yellow cast but comes in shades from gold to white. Blacklip, or black back oyster, goes from grey to white. The pearl oyster was used for flat pieces, the pure white mother-of-pearl for the best quality work. Abalone is the green-blue shell which can be very thinly sliced and is often used for flat-sided boxes. Lastly there is a pink tinged oyster shell.[6] Mother-of-pearl needs a classical design to set off the gleaming material; it does not lend itself well to novelties or toys.

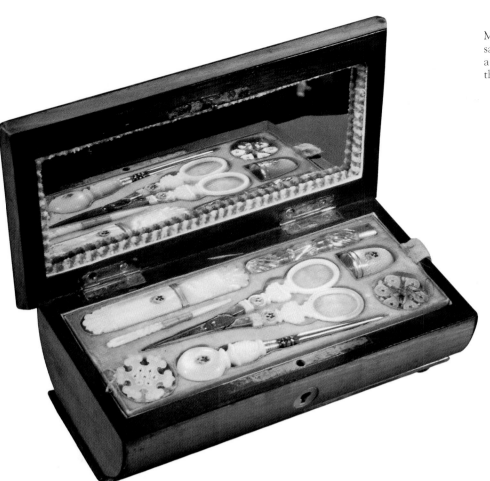

Mother-of-pearl Palais Royal sewing set in a satinwood box, approximately 8" long, containing a needle case, stiletto, winders, scissors, and a thimble. $2,240/£1,400.

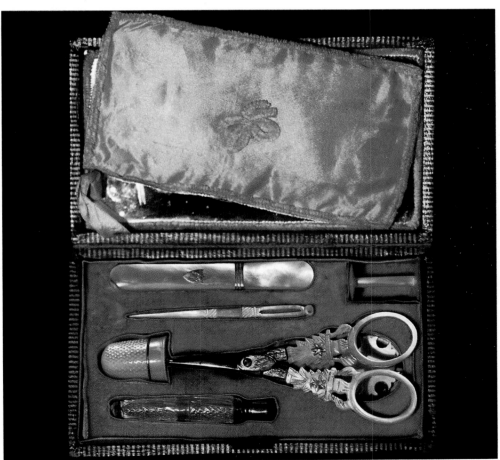

Palais Royal sewing set in a tooled leather box, approximately 8" long. Note the Spitalfields silk cushion bound with silk chenille. $2,240/£1,400.

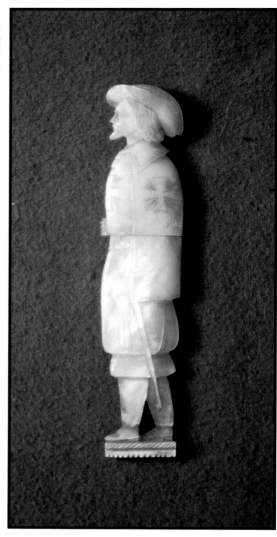

Mother-of-pearl needle case
with a central opening
showing the figure of a
cavalier. Approximately
$640/£400.

The legendary Palais Royal
thimble with central pansy
in enamel. $880/£550.

Mother-of-pearl Palais Royal
needle case in the form of a dog,
central opening. Approximately
$560/£350.

Mother-of-pearl needle case made as the figure of a Commedia del Arte character. Approximately $640/£400.

Mother-of-pearl needle case in the figure of a man, plus three little wax holders and a winder. The green dyed ivory letters surrounding the figure were from an alphabet set used to teach children.

Toys, Compendiums, and Novelties
in the Eighteenth Century

As we have formerly explained the use of the word "toy" to mean "gift," *objets de vitrine,* or little collectibles, you will not confuse these items with playthings for children. An example of a "toy" in a sewing tool might be a miniature sewing set or a thimble that unscrews from its base to reveal a scent bottle. A toy is often the name given to a combination of two or more items. What a pleasing gift to receive at the turn of the century!

A compendium has an altogether more serious ring to it. A typical compendium might be a silver thimble on a stand. The stand has a seal for letters at the base and a needle case which unscrews from under the tiny powder container, which in turn is attached to the thimble atop. These compendiums are nearly always made in silver and it is important to see whether the same design appears on each piece. You may find a number scratched on the inside of the pieces which may have been to assist assembly.

The term novelty often means one item made in the form of another, for example a tape-measure in the form of a miniature lantern, or a thimble case that looks like a little hatbox. Samuel Pemberton is known to have made novelty thimble cases, typically decorated with bright cut engraving which gave the surface a sparkle. Joseph Taylor made novelty pin cushions, often in the shape of tiny flower baskets. Inside the swing handle you can sometimes find his mark, I.T. (as J was not used). Novelties are often made as an example of exuberant, virtuoso creativity on the part of the creator. They really came into their own in the nineteenth century, with famous makers such as Henry William Dee, who made delightful novelty sewing items in silver.

A silver compendium.
Approximately $1,000/£625.

The same compendium unscrewed to show each section containing a thimble, a tiny pierced powderer, a needle case, and a thread holder.

Two "toys," one in silver and one in ivory. Both thimbles unscrew to reveal tiny scent bottles. Each approximately $960/£600.

Shopping Areas

Where might you have bought these wonderful frivolities? In most eighteenth century cities, shopping areas were still clearly defined by the goods that they sold. In London, mercers and drapers were in Cheapside and Spitalfields, book-sellers in Little Britain, and seamstresses, lace and textile merchants in Paternoster Row. However, The Strand, Oxford Street, and Bond Street, which were the new shopping areas, offered shops selling all kinds of differing goods, including fine sewing tools. Josiah Wedgwood, the famous potter, had opened his first show room in Grosvenor Square, just off Oxford Street. Thimbles were among the eighteenth century Wedgwood factory inventory, but those found in today's collections come from the twentieth century. If early ones were ever made, therefore, none seem to have survived. Wedgwood plaques were certainly mounted on eighteenth century steel châtelaines.

Fitted sewing boxes and boxed sets, étuis, and novelty items could all be purchased from the smart new shops in London's "West End." A fitted sewing box with all the tools, was very much an eighteenth century invention. By the end of the Georgian period, boxes were beginning to get larger. Red-tooled Moroccan leather ones were popular, with their gilded brass mounts and animal-inspired pad or claw feet. Most boxes still had feet, which gives them a lighter, more elegant look, even if the feet were just simple, turned ivory balls. If you look on the bottom of some boxes, you can see holes where these feet once were. These can be replaced, either by using large ivory beads or by getting a woodturner to make you some suitable substitutes.

Tiny versions of bigger boxes were made, often to take needle packets. Miniature knife boxes were fashioned to take needles and a thimble. Some have ivory leaves to divide up the needle partitions, and these can be replaced if they are missing. Miniature red leather boxes were also made for needle packets and thimbles. Boxes of a similar nature, in descending sizes, can make a nice display. There are so many delightful little tools to collect, such as waxers, tools used to wax thread smooth for sewing silk or to stiffen the cotton to facilitate threading a needle.

Winders, Clamps, and Lucets

Winders, which on their own can make a fascinating collection, are much more varied than commonly imagined. They were used in work boxes to wind your thread around before cotton reels were invented. In the eighteenth century, you would find them made in silver filigree, glass, gold, tortoiseshell, ivory, painted wood—indeed any material you can think of. Because of their obvious resemblance, the tiny mother-of-pearl ones are often called snowflakes. When you purchased skeins of silk, you would take them home and wind the silk onto your winders, using your clamps. The cheapest variety of winders were made of cut card and edged with gilt paper. You can still find these at the bottom of old sewing boxes.

Clamps are interesting to collect too; they are amongst the most unusual tools. There are two sorts of clamps: the winding clamps which come in pairs and have cages on top (often found inside a smart eighteenth century sewing box), and the single variety. Winding clamps might be of cut steel, with sparkling steel decorations that look like diamonds when in mint condition. (If you have any early cut steel, do not keep handling it because that will cause it to rust.) You clamped them to the edge of your table, about six inches apart, then placed the silk skein over the cages, which turned as you wound. The process was just as you might do with a knitting wool skein around a friend's hands, which you wound into a ball.

The single clamp often had a pin cushion on the top, and perhaps a little drawer. These bigger clamps were nicknamed The Third Hand. You clamped your material to the side of the table and screwed it tight in the vice to give yourself a free hand with which to cut or pin.

Clamps were used right through the eighteenth century into the mid-nineteenth. The famous one that everyone has heard of is The Hemming Bird, which was made in the 1850s. If you look closely at the brass wing tip, you will sometimes find a patent number and the date of the patent, 1851. Apart from birds, many other animals were used in a decorative manner for clamps, even dogs—but those were nineteenth century follies! In the eighteenth century the predominant materials used were iron and steel.

If you find a small hook on your clamp, this would have been to hold the thread firm for netting. On early painted Tunbridge ware clamps, you may see a tape-measure, or thimble stump attached to the top. Clamps are amongst the most intricate of tools, whereas the lucet is one of the simplest. Lucets were made in wood and ivory, and there are rare examples in mother-of-pearl. Some have handles, but the majority are without. They were used to make cord and were employed in the eighteenth through the nineteenth century. The diameter of the cord depended on the thickness of the thread.

Top row: steel scissors, tambour hook, waxer and tape, silver filigree waxer, mother-of-pearl and gold thimble case on a chain. Bottom row: Samuel Pemberton silver needle case with bright cut decoration, mother-of-pearl quiver needle case, winder, and a silver filigree tape-measure.

Hooks and Pin-balls

Tambour hooks and crochet hooks were used in the eighteenth and the nineteenth centuries. Tambour work was a popular Georgian craft, practiced in the main by ladies of means. The word *tambour* comes from the French word for drum, because the frame is round and made of wood, resembling a military drum. A tambour hook is small, sharp, and pointed, because it has to pierce the net and hook the thread through. The hook is secured by a butterfly screw in steel at the side. The handle can be made from a great variety of materials, such as tortoiseshell, ivory, mother-of-pearl, or gold. The end that protects the hook should be unscrewed and then screwed onto the other end to give greater length and balance to the handle. There are often extra hooks in a cavity in the handle.

Pin-balls are a very typical late eighteenth century item. They were usually finely knitted, often dated, and sometimes bore motifs of flowers or animals. Very fine ones are sometimes mounted in silver, similar to those made in the seventeenth century, although this was mainly a continental fashion. The balls were made in two halves, stuffed very firmly, then sewn up with a cord to cover the join. The cord could then be used to hang the pin-ball from your belt.

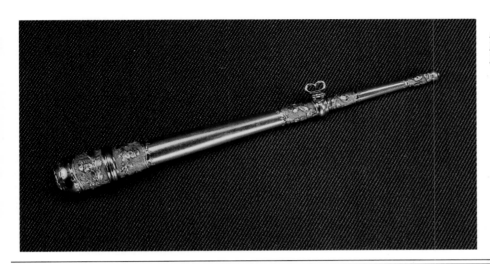

A gold tambour hook, Paris 1763. *Courtesy of S. J. Phillips Ltd., Antique Silver and Jewelry of New Bond Street, London.*

Dieppe Work

Some of the loveliest groups of ivory tools are often given the umbrella name of Dieppe work. It would be hard to tell if all given that name had originally been carved in Dieppe, a French seaside town and port on the Normandy coast. As long ago as the fourteenth century the town was importing large quantities of ivory from West Africa. By the early seventeenth century ivory carving was a flourishing industry and the English and Dutch visitors were eager to buy the exquisite creations made by the "Dieppe Carvers." Sewing tools—needle cases, pin cushions, thimbles, tape-measures, netting sets, clamps, and winders—would be made from the smaller off-cuts of ivory tusks used for bigger carvings.

Dieppe work is used as a generic term to describe a certain style of carving, recognizable by a depth and crispness of detail and a naturalness of execution. The flowers appear to be alive, the fruit waiting to be eaten. The flowers arranged in baskets concealed a tape-measure, a cornucopia spilling over with fruit opened to reveal a needle case. The famous fisher folk needle cases are now rare, especially in good condition, but you can occasionally find similar pairs of figures in wood and silver. I was lucky enough to find a silver pair in the antique shop in Charles de Gaulle airport. The silver figures were wearing slightly more refined clothes than their ivory cousins. Some souvenir pieces were inscribed with the word "Dieppe."

Sewing Boxes

Very elaborate sewing boxes from Paris, fitted out with every conceivable tool, were the height of elegant sophistication at the end of the eighteenth century and into the nineteenth. Some had painted porcelain lids that opened to reveal gold tools, some had whole shells for lids with pearl, silver, and ivory fittings. Other boxes were made in the shape of a pianoforte, with a musical movement concealed in the bottom. Ivory boxes with ivory tools, both decorated with black lac work and made in India for export, came in from Vizagapatam.[6] Ivory boxes fitted out with 18 ct. gold tools were imported from the Petrabgarh[7] workshops in Rasputana in North India. The typical Petrabgarh work has pierced gold designs of flowers and tiny animals, backed with red or green mica. Ivory was shipped over regularly by the East India Company and was the most favored material for a fitted sewing box until the 1840s.

If you could not afford an expensive box, there were many attractive alternatives. Scroll work boxes were mainly homemade; you could buy the carcass, then cut tiny strips of paper, roll them into scrolls and shapes, and stick them onto the box. Pen work looks like a print or engraving, but was often done just using pen and ink. This could be done at home, as there were many talented amateur artists.

Tortoiseshell

Tortoiseshell sewing boxes and tools have always been amongst the favorites. Very much in vogue in the 1830s, the boxes retained much of the Regency elegance and lightness. This is partly due to the boxes having feet, which were to vanish later on. The feet were predominantly ivory, and the shape of the box was often borrowed from a classical sarcophagus. The carcass was cheap wood with sheets of tortoiseshell glued on, then trimmed with ivory. The tools inside were sometimes ivory, mother-of-pearl, or silver. Tortoiseshell boxes and tools are still some of the most sought after and expensive. It is a material no longer available to us, and fairly fragile, so little remains in good condition. Most boxes were made in the 1830s, when the large shells were being brought over to Europe. Tortoiseshell can be polished if the surface looks dull from wear, but it must be done professionally.

Smaller items in tortoiseshell, such as needle cases shaped liked little knife boxes, are always delightful, and expensive. A tortoiseshell thimble in good condition, made by the firm of Piercy and often referred to as a Piercy's Patent, could set you back $3200 (£2000). When the shell is inlaid with silver or gold, called piqué work, it is even more desirable. You may find small items in piqué in the bottom of your work box, such as little purses, buttons, or even jewelry. Winders in shell are rare but very occasionally you might find a set of spools to hold thread. Blond tortoiseshell was always the most expensive. By 1990 it had become so rare that it was more expensive than gold. In Paris, it fetched 100 francs a gram, when gold was 90 francs. Blond shell was used by the Japanese to make the glowing eyes of the little animals featured in shibayama work. If you see any shell, buy it even if the article is damaged, in case you ever need any for a repair.

Tortoiseshell tools are expensive, but pin-poppets, pin cases, pin cushions, and pins are within most collectors' pockets. Pins were still used in enormous quantities, packaged by prisoners in the state prisons in London and then distributed under a trade name to the retailers.[8] Very occasionally it is possible to find early silver pin boxes from the seventeenth and eighteenth centuries, but these are rare items, and usually turn up in silver auctions.

Sewing box in blonde and flame tortoiseshell inlaid with mother-of-pearl. $3,200/£2,000.

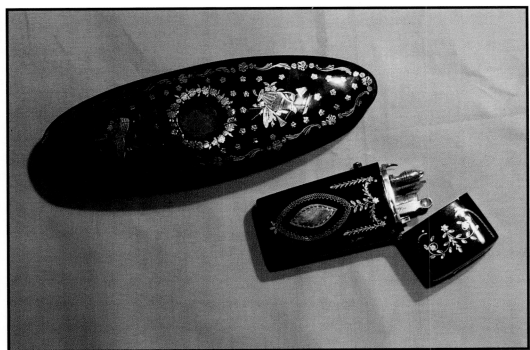

Top: a tortoiseshell knotting shuttle decorated with piqué (which is an inlay of silver and/or gold). There is a central mirror, perhaps to keep an eye on how one looked as one carried on knotting. Approximately $800/£500. Bottom: a small tortoiseshell étui, containing scissors, penknife, tweezers, ear spoon, and ivory notebook. $960/£600.

Tortoiseshell étui, with scissors, ivory notebook, scent bottle, and tweezers. $800/£500.

Three needle cases, two in tortoiseshell inlaid with silver and gold, the third metal covered in leather, mounted with steel. $320-480/£200-300 each.

Rare curved tortoiseshell and gold needle case. $800/£500.

Carved tortoiseshell netting case and tools. The fine knitted cover was made by the current owner who is a surgeon. Watching over his wife, who was seriously ill for a long time, he found doing this fine work relaxing. Approximately $40/£25. *Courtesy of Arca, Grays Antiques of Daris Street.*

Changing Manufacturing Practices

Spitalfields silk was used to line boxes and sets, to make tape-measures and cover pin cushions. It is worth collecting scraps of old fabric for sympathetic repairs. Next time you look at a box, notice the beautiful embroidered and padded covers and linings, and the fine silk chenille trimmings. In boxed sets, there are often padded, silk velvet pin cushions embroidered with gold thread, tiny sequins, and colorful flower sprays. Worked handkerchiefs, interior cushions for boxes, and ribbon weaving were the simplest part of the textile trade and mainly done by women and children. Ribbon work was used to make the flowers on the pads inside sewing sets. This work was carried out at home, on very low pay. It was these out workers who were the first to suffer in a recession.

The East End of London around Spitalfields was still scattered with Huguenot families, one of the most famous being the Courtaulds. Louisa Perina Courtauld took over her husband's goldsmith business after his death in 1770, ensuring its prosperity. Later on the business grew to include textiles, for which it is still famous today. Business enterprises were burgeoning all over the capital. During the eighteenth century, London's population doubled, from approximately half a million to one million by 1800. Industrial inventiveness was encouraged by the increase in disposable income.

John Kay invented the flying shuttle in 1733, enabling a far broader cloth to be woven. The distaff and spindle method of spinning was slow, and so was the spinning wheel, so in 1741 John Wyatt invented successive pairs of rollers. Together with Lewis Paul, he opened the first mill in Birmingham. Then the spinning jenny was invented by James Hargreaves, who patented his design in Nottingham in 1770. Samuel Crompton had the brilliant idea of combining the Wyatt rollers with Hargreaves' jenny, enabling him to produce a yarn of fineness never before achieved in Britain. The sound of the spinning wheel in cottages all over the British countryside was soon to die away.

There is often a price to be paid for inventions that achieve greater perfection and cut down on the use of manpower. Unemployment caused widespread poverty, and, as always, it hit hardest those who had the least resources. For the first time, the pawnshop served as the poor people's only recourse to money during hard times, becoming a widespread and recognized phenomenon. The sign of the three golden balls came originally from the coat of arms of the Medici, the famous Renaissance family of Florence. The Medici family, especially Lorenzo, were great patrons of the Arts and later became powerful bankers. The Medici sign was appropriated by pawnbrokers to imbue an air of tradition and probity to their enterprises. Many an unemployed seamstress took her tools there in times of hardship. To this day, there is still a regular sale at Phillips of unreclaimed pawnbrokers' goods; many a gold or silver thimble, or châtelaine, has been sold there.

Victory in the Seven Years War gave Britain mastery of the oceans and provided the financial impetus for the approaching Industrial Revolution. This enabled Britain to become a great exporter of goods the world over. America had been born as a new nation, encompassing the ideals of democracy, and an American identity in manufacture and design was beginning to develop. At the turn of the century, Europe was starting to be dominated by Napoleon, so French designs in all things, including sewing tools, were considered the apogee of elegance. Today it seems contradictory to be constantly concerned with possible invasion from a country, while at the same time admiring its artistic taste! "Made in Paris" was embossed on the fine sewing sets that most elegant women wanted to display. French sewing tools have a special lightness and delicacy; their ornamentation never seems to overburden the form and shape of the tool.

Women in the early 1800s were leading the way in all branches of the sewing trade. At last the power of the guilds was evaporating, and women made lingerie, hats, shirts, bed linen, shoes, fans, and bags. They crocheted, painted on porcelain and enamel, etched, engraved, and generally did many highly skilled jobs in areas not previously open to them. If you can imagine all the sewing tools that must have been needed, it is no wonder that the simple brass thimbles from the end of the eighteenth century are found in some quantity. Plain but well made, razor-sharp steel scissors are still to be had and bone crochet hooks remain cheap. In tandem with exquisite sewing tools, many decorated by women, look for the simpler tools of the working seamstress. These can form an interesting collection too, and are certainly cheaper for the novice to start off with.

The end of the eighteenth century and the beginning of the nineteenth saw the gradual softening of the two-class system. The earlier tradition of an aristocracy, who depended on land for their wealth, and a peasantry, who worked on and around the great estates, was giving ground to a rising third class, the middle class. This is evident when looking at the sewing tools and related artifacts. Under the Georgian kings, there was still a marked division between the very refined tools used for pleasure and fashion, and those more robust tools used for necessity. The expanding commerce of England was creating a thriving middle class, people who depended on business rather than land for their income. That middle class created a market for leisured pastimes, many of which involved some form of needlework. The nineteenth century was definitely the period of greatest wealth and commercial productivity in Britain.

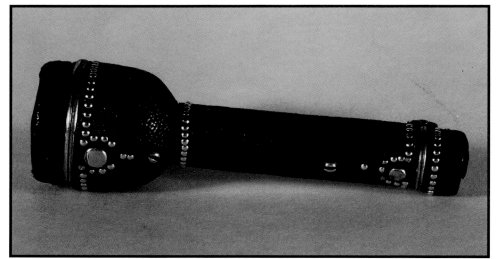

Opposite page:
A collection of needle holders and
bodkins, mainly eighteenth century,
but the leather items and walnut are
c. 1800-1830.

Black shagreen combination
needle and thimble case
decorated with little gold nails,
similar to *Clouté* work (see page
126). $640/£400.

Selected tools. Top row: gold
and enamel thimble (note the
Palais Royal pansy plaque) and
two gold thimbles. Bottom row:
gold and turquoise set needle
case, plus silver scissors in a
sheath (all nineteenth century).

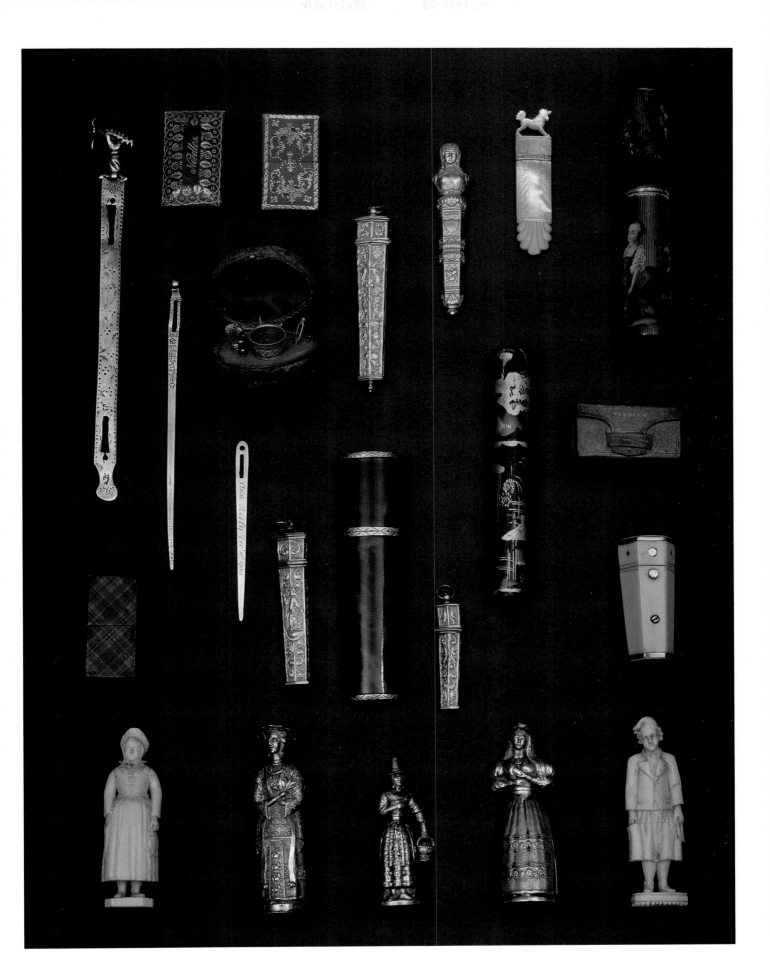

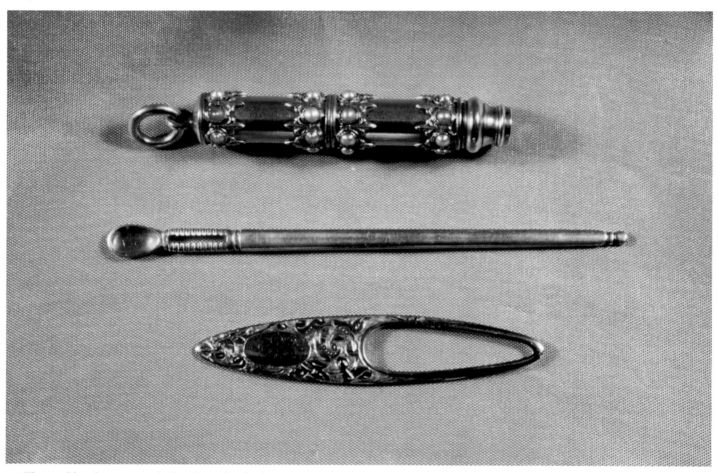

Three gold tools: a pencil inlaid with pearls, a bodkin
combined with an ear spoon, and ribbon threader.

A Meissen thimble, c. 1760. Approximately $4,800-8,000/£3,000-5,000.

A selection of châtelaines and scissors cases, with a compendium in the center.

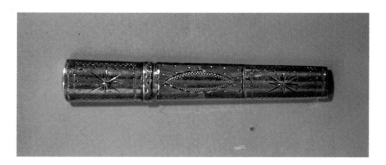

A silver needle case by John Tolekin (or Toleken), 84 Grand Parade. He was naturalized in 1768 as a foreign merchant and worked as a silversmith until 1836. Registered 1798.

Silver thimble case and thimble, late eighteenth century. The case is delicately engraved all over. $560/£350.

A Cantonese carved ivory netting set. $480/£300.

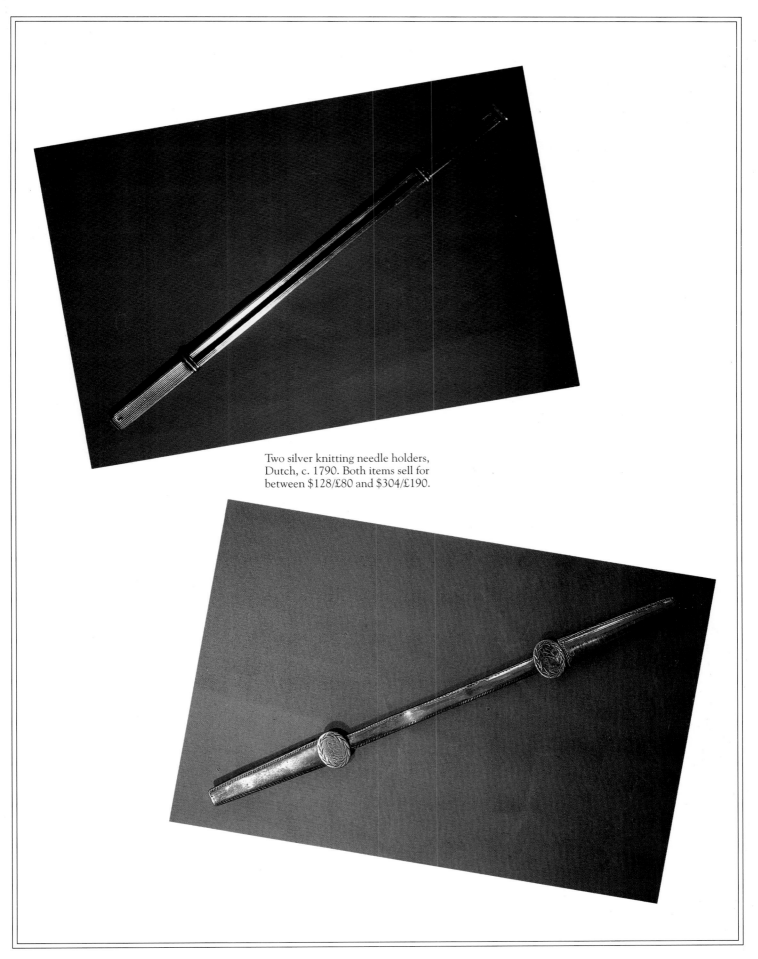

Two silver knitting needle holders,
Dutch, c. 1790. Both items sell for
between $128/£80 and $304/£190.

A very fine Swedish gold set of two finger guards and a central thimble. On both sides of the finger guard the maker's marks and initials are engraved. $4,800/£3,000.

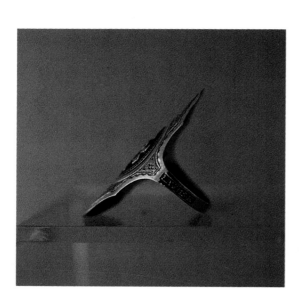

Side view of the two finger guards, showing the maker's marks and initials.

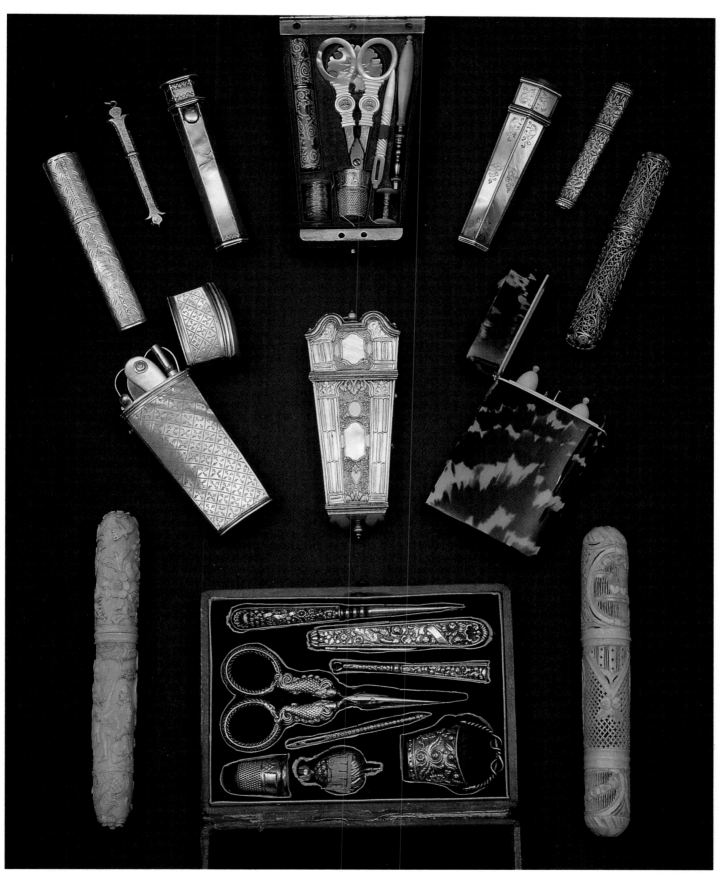

A selection of fitted cases and needle holders. The bottom box, fitted with silver tools, is early nineteenth century.

An opaline (possibly alabaster) hand-painted hand cooler, to hold in your hand to cool on the stone.

A selection of tools, including needle cases, scissors, thimble, and thimble toys which unscrew to reveal little scent bottles.

Chapter Five

The Nineteenth Century

At the beginning of this century, the fashionable styles were the Empire in France and the Regency in England. Europe was in turmoil during the Napoleonic wars, but Britain became cautiously optimistic after the Battle of Waterloo in 1815. The Regency style was marked by an elegant refinement—but often using inexpensive materials. If precious metals were used, the silver and gold content was light. Many English techniques were used in the manufacture of sewing tools that catered to a less wealthy, but still discerning, market. Simple materials such as wood, straw, and bone were employed, combined with a high standard of workmanship.

Working Women and the Sewing Trade

When Queen Victoria ascended the throne in 1837, Britain was becoming one of the world's most prosperous nations; that is one reason why we have so many antiques and sewing tools from that period available in such a variety of materials. Due to the English enjoyment of travel, and the extra money they now had jingling in their pockets, there are probably more good French sewing sets in Britain than in France. Sadly the prosperity did not reach the poorer classes, especially those employed in branches of the textile trade. Their plight was expressed poetically by Thomas Hood in *The Shirtmaker* (1843):

> Stitch, stitch, stitch
> In poverty hunger and dirt,
> Sewing at once with a double thread,
> A shroud as well as a shirt

Postcard showing a photograph of Queen Victoria and Prince Albert, c. 1860.

Earning your living by plying your needle in the early part of Queen Victoria's reign was only one step away from prostitution, as the wages were below subsistence level. When we look at collections of sewing tools, we skip over the working variety as being too ordinary to bother with, yet so much of human life is there. Two collections side by side would make an interesting comparison. Each century has had its tools of necessity and those of luxury, but in the nineteenth century we have the introduction of those used by the middle classes. The power of the middle classes grew as the century progressed. It was still a period of uneven distribution of wealth, but writers such as Mayhew, Dickens, and Mrs. Gaskell were battling to increase awareness of the plight of the chronically poor. Henry Mayhew, for example, author of *London Labour and the London Poor* (1851), wrote the following letter, later published in *The Unknown Mayhew: Selections from the Morning Chronicle:*

Postcard showing a study for *The Sempstress* (1844), by Richard Redgrave.

Prostitution among Needlewomen (1849)

I had no idea of the intensity of the privations suffered by the needlewomen of London until I came to enquire into this part of the subject. But the poor creatures shall speak for themselves; here is one account, typical of many, her story is as follows:

"I make moleskin trowsers. I get 7p. and 8p. per pair. I can do two pairs in a day, and twelve when there is full employment, in a week. But some weeks I have no work at all. I work from six in the morning to ten at night; that is what I call my day's work. When I am fully employed I get from 7s. to 8s. a week. My expenses out of that for twist, thread, and candles are about 1s.6p. a week, leaving me about 6s. per week clear. But there's coals to pay for out of this, and that's at the least 6p. more; so 5s.6p. is the very outside of what I earn when I'm in full work. Lately, I have been dreadfully slack; so we are every winter, all of us "sloppers," and that's the time when we wants the most money. The week before last I had but two pair to make all week; so that I only earnt 1s. clear. For this last month I'm sure I haven't done any more than that each week. Taking one week with another, all the year round I don't make above 3s. clear money each week. I don't work at any other kind of slop-work. The trowsers work is held to be the best paid of all. I give 1s. a week rent.

"My father died when I was five years of age. My mother is a widow, upwards of 66 years of age, and seldom has a day's work. Generally once in the week she is employed pot-scouring - that is, cleaning publicans' pots. She is paid 4p. a dozen for that, and does about four dozen and a half, so that she gets about 1s.6p. in the day by it. For the rest she is dependent upon me. I am 20 years of age the 25th of this month. We earn together, to keep the two of us, from 4s.6p. to 5s. each week. Out of this we have to pay 1s. rent, and there remains 3s.6p. to 4s. to find us both in food and clothing. It is of course impossible for us to live upon it, and the consequence is I am obliged to go a bad way. I have been three years working at slop-work.

"I was virtuous when I first went to work, and I remained so till this last twelvemonth. I struggled very hard to keep myself chaste, but I found that I couldn't get food and clothing for myself and mother, so I took to live with a young man. He is turned 20. He is a tinman. He did promise to marry me, but his sister made mischief between me and him, so that parted us. I have not seen him now for about six months, and I can't say whether he will keep his promise or not. I am now pregnant by him, and expect to be confined in two months' time. He knows of my situation, and so does my mother. My mother believed me to be married to him. She knows otherwise now. I was very fond of him, and had known him for about two years before he seduced me. He could make 14s. a week. He told me if I came to live with him he'd take care I shouldn't want, and both mother and me had been very bad off before. He said, too, he'd make me his lawful wife, but I hardly cared so long as I could get food for myself and mother.

"Many young girls at the shop advised me to go wrong. They told me how comfortable they was off; they said they could get plenty to eat and drink, and good clothes. There wasn't one young girl as can get her living by slop-work. The masters all know this, but they wouldn't own to it of course. It stands to reason that no one can live and pay rent, and find clothes, upon 3s. a week, which is the most they can make clear, even the best hands, at the moleskin and cord trowsers work. There's poor people moved out of our house that was making 3/4p. shirts. I am satisfied there is not one young girl that works at slop-work that is virtuous, and there are some thousands in the trade. They may do very well if they have got mothers and fathers to find them a home and food, and to let them have what they earn for clothes; then they may be virtuous, but not without. I've heard of numbers who have gone from slop-work to the streets altogether for a living, and I shall be obliged to do the same thing myself unless something better turns up for me.

"If I was never allowed to speak no more, it was the little money I got by my labour that led me to go wrong. Could I have honestly earnt enough to have subsisted upon, to find me in proper food and clothing, such as is necessary, I should not have gone astray; no, never. As it was, I fought against it as long as I could - that I did - to the last. I hope to be able to get a ticket for a midwife; a party has promised me as much, and, he says, if possible, he'll get me an order for a box of linen. My child will only increase my burdens, and if my young man won't support my child I must go on the streets altogether. I know how horrible all this is. It would have been much better for me to have subsisted upon a dry crust and water rather than be as I am now. But no one knows the temptations of us poor girls in want. Gentlefolks can never understand it. If I had been born a lady it wouldn't have been very hard to have acted like one. To be poor and to be honest, especially with young girls, is the hardest struggle of all. There isn't one in a thousand that can get the better of it. I am ready to say again, that it was want, and nothing more, that made me transgress. If I had been better paid I should have done better. Young as I am, my life is a curse to me. If the ALMIGHTY WOULD PLEASE TO TAKE ME BEFORE MY CHILD IS BORN, I SHOULD DIE HAPPY."

Almost fifteen years later in the workrooms of Madam Elise, a London court dressmaker, a young seamstress was found dead on 17th June 1863, her death directly related to her working conditions (Museum of London archive). Working by gaslight in badly ventilated and overcrowded rooms, such workers had little to eat and no rest or exercise, yet were expected to work a fourteen-hour day, extended during the season to seventeen hours or more. Completion of dresses was often demanded twenty-four hours after ordering. Despite this, the employment offered women respectability and some chance of advancement. Even though Britain was the wealthiest Empire the world had ever known, the ripples on the lake of plenty had not extended far enough to lap at the feet of the poor. Women's work was at the bottom of the pile, especially in sewing affiliated trades; it paid a pauper's wage.

The sewing tools used by our poor young seamstress, let us call her Elsie, would have been made in simple undecorated brass or steel. Needles would be in their paper packets, from the Redditch needle makers. Leading needle manufacturers of the time were Able Morall and H.Milward & Son, J.W. Lewis, and of course the famous W. Avery & Son. Our Elsie would not have been able to afford one of the Avery novelty cases, so popular in the 1860s and 1870s. To research and enjoy their variety, read *Victorian Brass Needle-cases* by Estelle Horowitz and Ruth Mann. Elsie might have had a mother at home who was a sock knitter, as that paid a few pennies. Tools needed were knitting needles, perhaps some needle end-protectors and a yarn hook or spool knave on your belt. If you were nursing a baby, you could keep one hand free by using a knitting sheath. According to Edward Pinto, only eight seventeenth century sheaths exist to his knowledge, but they were abundant during the Victorian era. Knitting needle châtelaines, suspended from the belt and with a hook for the yarn, would have been used by middle class women.

An Avery needle case in the form of an artist's easel, more likely to be used by middle class women than by the working class seamstresses. Approximately $208/£130.

Button making was another working woman's trade. You covered a metal base with linen, then overworked it with a tracery of fine thread. The wages enabled a family to live when it had lost its breadwinner. Cards of linen-covered buttons in different sizes were made for vests, shirts, and petticoats, with the smallest being an eighth of an inch (3mm); literally thousands were needed. Then John Aston demonstrated his button-making machine at the Great Exhibition in 1851 and near starvation hit some families. In the bottom of old sewing boxes you can find evidence of many lowly paid occupations for women. You might find buttons made from the horn of Dorset sheep in the nineteenth century, for example. This was another cottage industry for farmers' wives.

Rummage further, and some paper twists of beads appear, so fine that they were known as sand (sable) for sable work, which was the finest beading used to cover all manner of sewing tools such as needle and thimble cases. Tiny shells may be discovered too, ready to be glued onto souvenir pin cushions from a day at the seaside, reached by traveling on one of those new trains. You might find paper figures in old yellowing envelopes; these were cut out of periodicals to stick onto *papier mâché* sewing boxes. Ribbons ruched and ready for ribbon flowers were made up to sew onto the needle-books. Fish scales were kept in little boxes, to make into flower petals, attached like sequins. Of course not all this work was done for sale; much was done for personal domestic use. Stiffened gauze would have been made ready to embroider with cross-stitch for a crochet hook case. Bristol Board,[1] a perforated stiffened paper, is still waiting for somebody's needle to make it into a bookmark. Perhaps it bears a charming homily—already printed to stitch over—advising one to "think of the giver," or perhaps a timid message of affection never sent.

Symbolism in Sewing

Much symbolism was used to send secret personal messages. In an age when strict rules of protocol were observed between the sexes, naturally every means under the sun was sought to circumnavigate them. A sewing box was the perfect hiding place. Many a shy suitor might start off by giving the object of his affection a thimble inscribed "Forget me not," a gift which would not be considered compromising, whereas to accept jewelry would be improper unless engaged. Lace bobbins with "Love me more than all the boys," inscribed in a spiral of tenderness, might be given by a farmhand to the dairymaid. Every flower had a different meaning: a rosebud signifying pure love might be embroidered alongside a pious motto, then given as a prayer-book marker to the young curate. We are all familiar with the forget-me-not, but not as much with the yellow rose, which can signify adultery—a horticultural hazard for the unaware!

Ivory pin cushion with a message to "Esteem the Giver."

Sewing in the Forces

Soldiers used to sew and embroider "Pockets" for their girlfriends to hang on the wall. They were made from the red felt of an old uniform and often decorated with a regimental badge. Beads from their tours of duty in India would be sewn on, as well as gold thread from old badges, foreign shells, and anything else that took their fancy. Sometimes you find a Tudor rose, a harp, or a thistle, embroidered on as symbols of Britain. Pockets are rare, and will fetch high prices, equivalent to that of a sampler.

A soldier's "pocket," principally made from the red felt taken from a military coat and then embroidered with various symbols such as a crown, a cross, regimental badges, and an Irish harp at the bottom, early nineteenth century. The beads come from India, probably from a tour of duty. Approximately $960/£600.

A further example of a pocket, also in military red felt and embroidered with scissors, a thimble, and the words "a present" at the bottom. $368/£230.

A pin cushion matching the pocket shown below.

A gold work and sequined eighteenth century pocket, made for a wedding trousseau.

Postcard showing a portrait of
Emma, Lady Hamilton,
Nelson's mistress, c. 1800

A portrait of Admiral Nelson.
*Courtesy of the Royal Maritime
Museum, Greenwich.*

Sailors have always been famous for their *Scrimshaw* work, that is, the carving and decorating of whale and animal bones. The anchor was often engraved, as a symbol of constancy. Many items were made, including needle cases and very occasionally thimbles, which were then sent home as presents. Unfortunately, much of this scrimshaw work has been copied and more is being made now. The Inuit people still carry on their tradition of carved and decorated bone, even making a sort of châtelaine joined by leather or cord with hollowed-out bone pendants.

Emma, Lady Hamilton, who is famous for being the lover of Admiral Lord Nelson, was a wonderful needlewoman. If you visit The Maritime Museum at Greenwich in England, ask to see the cot hangings that she made for Nelson on board ship. They are not on permanent view, but may be seen if you telephone in advance. Emma also embroidered the hems of her dresses with symbols of Nelson's victories. After one battle, she waited for him on the quay, her beautiful gown embroidered with a border of acorns, acorn leaves, and anchors (these symbols referred to the ballad "Hearts of Oak," celebrating Nelson's warships that won victories at Lagos, Quebec, and Quiberon). Fragments are in the archives. There are also cambric squares and napkins embroidered by Lady Nelson, his lawful wife.

Trafalgar chintz was brought out directly after Nelson's death, with emblems of palm trees and his last signal of "England expects every man to do his duty" printed on it. The design can be viewed in the archives. There is also a sailor's little sewing hussif (a portable sewing set) on view in the Museum, and Sir Thomas Masterman Hardy's purse made out of bead work. Army officers were always issued with sewing kits, right up to the last war. Ones that survive from the early nineteenth century are in gold tooled, Moroccan leather, unfolding like a purse, with long sections to hold repairing silks. Some collectors confine their collections to items that are linked to the military—it is a good way to enlist the interest and support of a male spouse!

Lady Hamilton might have learned to sew on a sampler similar to this one.

Embroidery samples done by Emma,
Lady Hamilton. *Courtesy of the Royal
Maritime Museum, Greenwich.*

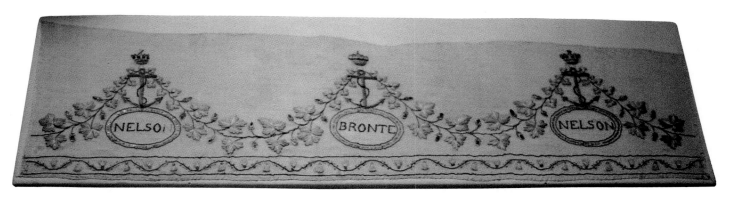

An embroidered hem, made and worn by Lady Hamilton in honor of
Nelson's victory. *Courtesy of the Royal Maritime Museum, Greenwich.*

Handkerchiefs embroidered by Lady Nelson, Lord Nelson's
wife. *Courtesy of the Royal Maritime Museum, Greenwich.*

Embroidery done by Lady Nelson, and her likeness.
Courtesy of the Royal Maritime Museum, Greenwich.

Beaded purse purported to have
belonged to Sir Thomas Masterman
Hardy. *Courtesy of the Royal Maritime
Museum, Greenwich.*

Sewing Boxes

Men might sail the seas, bringing home riches from the Empire, but most women stayed at home. This was the period of the large, sedate sewing box, rather like Queen Victoria, who would not be moved! (When she died, being very short and extremely stout, she was virtually a complete square!) Most of the sewing boxes no longer had feet. Although every conceivable kind of box was made, most were fitted out in fashionable mother-of-pearl. Six to eight cotton reel holders with mother-of-pearl tops were arranged at the side. There was often a mirror inside the lid that concealed a partition for letters. There were compartments for everything: a tape-measure, needle case, thimble, emery, waxer, scent bottle, and maybe some manicure instruments thrown in. Everything was kept in its allotted place, seemingly synonymous with the general attitude to Victorian mores. The boxes were in the main heavy, not to be carried around, pieces of solid furniture. From c. 1850 to the end of the century, sewing boxes were made to stay put.

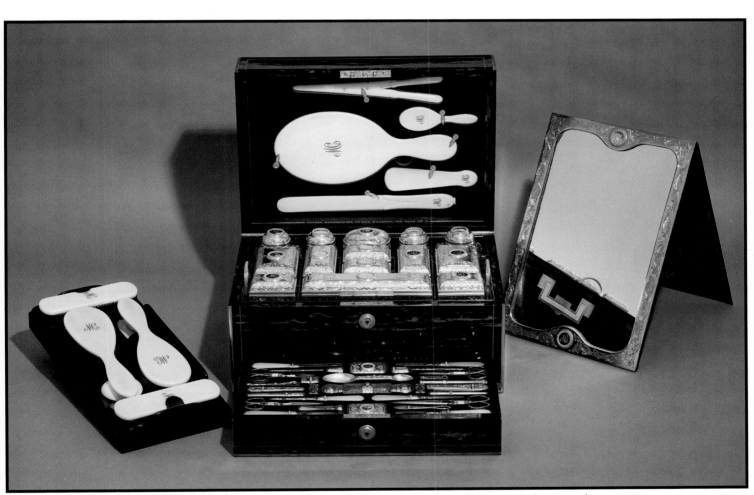

Mid-nineteenth century traveling box fitted with every conceivable accessory. Sewing tools in one tray, manicure and writing implements in another tray, and all things necessary for the toilet in the top. Silver-gilt set with turquoise in a rosewood box.

William IV mother-of-pearl fitted box in the manner of A.J. Strachan, fitted with gilt metal and enamel implements all with matching motif of snakes, c. 1835.

Sewing implements from inside the mother-of-pearl box on page 78.

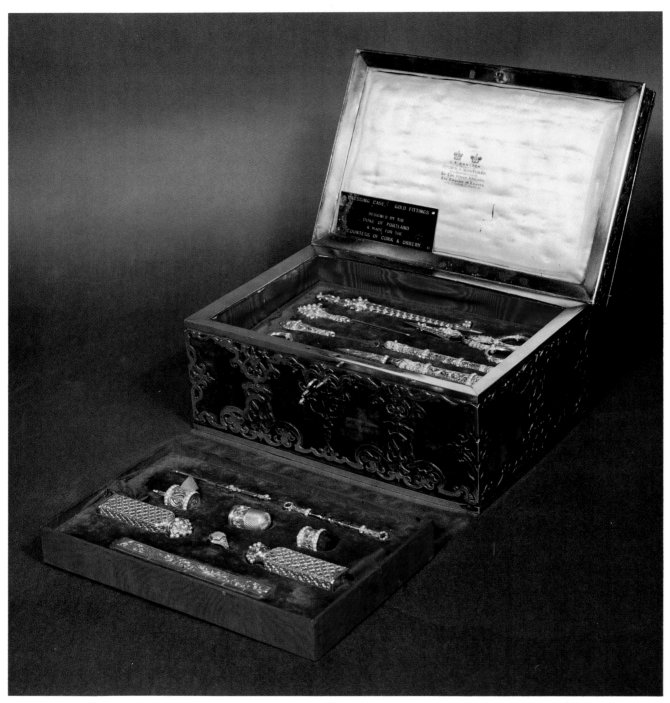

Early nineteenth century sewing box, all 18 ct. gold fitments. *Courtesy of John Jaffa.*

Châtelaines, Étuis, and Sewing Sets
in the Nineteenth Century

There were other ways of transporting your tools, rather than in a heavy sewing box. The châtelaine enjoyed yet another revival, very much part of the Pre-Raphaelites' admiration of an earlier age of romance. This time the chains were much longer, with three, five or more pendants. Items might include a thimble case, scissors case, emery, needle case, scent bottle, or a notebook and pencil. Silver was the predominant metal, but silver-plate, steel, and brass were all in demand. An étui, on the other hand, is a single container in which a variety of items is held; it can be portable, for carrying in a pocket, or simply kept on a table, like a smaller sewing box. Étui cases were often elaborately decorated and could be made of gold or silver. In the 1880s the leather-boxed sewing set, or *nécessaire*, was extremely popular throughout Europe. A nécessaire is a general term covering any small container, including a sewing box. The La-

dies Companion, yet another version of a sewing container, was upright with a deep lid, which on removal disclosed sewing tools fitted into compartments.

Châtelaines have the longest ancestry of all these accessories: their history can be traced back to Norman times. Over the years they have fallen in and out of fashion. A man's version, the *Macaroni*, was particularly popular with eighteenth century dandies; it was commonly worn in pairs, on either side, attached to the belt. A wide variety of châtelaines appeared throughout the nineteenth century, from the Romantic period of the 1810s (when Medieval and Renaissance revival designs of gold, pinchbeck, cut steel, and silver were made), to the time of the Great Exhibition of 1851 (where these "amusing little trifles" were noted with wry amusement by a writer in the *Illustrated London News*), to the 1890s (when cut-steel and silver versions proliferated).[2] It is not necessary to purchase only châtelaines that have all matching pendants: some were bought complete, others were added to as required.

An eighteenth century portrait
in oils of an elegant woman
wearing a double châtelaine
from her belt.

Silver-plate châtelaine decorated with cupids, flowers, and gardening tools in its original leather case, mid-nineteenth century. $2,560/£1,600.

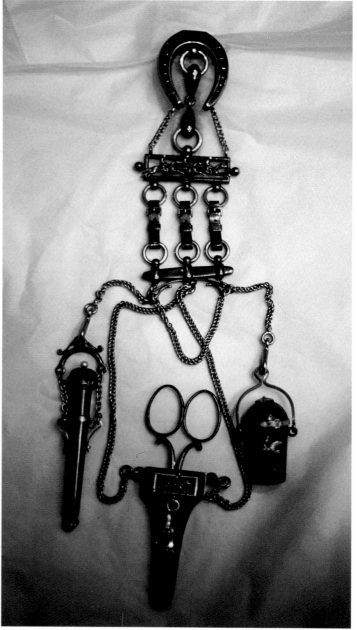

Steel gun-metal châtelaine (note the blue sheen) with equestrian motifs, mid-nineteenth century. *Private Collection.*

Turkish symbols appear on this
silver clip decorated with gold
moons, c. 1860. $320/£200.

A silver-plate châtelaine, late
nineteenth century. $560/£350.

A steel châtelaine with a little purse and a plate châtelaine hung with miniature daggers. Some of these "daggers" house miniature folding scissors, which were used by gentlemen to trim their moustaches and eyebrows. They were sometimes suspended singly from gentlemen's watch-chains. $720/£450.

Silver châtelaine with a waxer, pencil, notebook, scissors, thimble case, and emery. $1,200/£750.

Late nineteenth century miniature set of six pendants hanging from a bar, which can be worn as a brooch.

Unusual silver and gold decorated watch châtelaine, made in Paris in 1850. $560/£350.

A steel châtelaine, perhaps for a housekeeper or a young person. $640/£400.

Another steel example, with a purse, pin pad, whistle, notebook, scent bottle, corkscrew for scent bottles, knife, pin wheel, seam presser or pleater, charm, pencil and scissors. $960/£600.

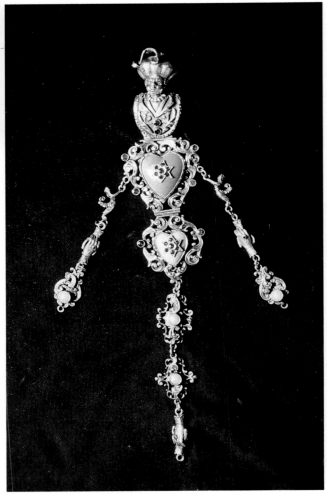

A châtelaine made to celebrate an Egyptian event which could relate to the discovery of the source of the Nile (see chronology) or the opening of a particular tomb. *Courtesy of Mr. L. Gould, Fine Collectors Objects and Enamels, Portobello Road, London.*

Russian, mid-nineteenth century châtelaine in silver with rose enamel and paste.

Lacquered box inlaid with rose colored gold, c. 1830. $960/£600.

Inside view showing the tools in silver gilt.

Blue opaline glass, probably French, made to resemble an egg in a bird's nest, c. 1850. It opens to reveal gilt metal tools. $800/£500.

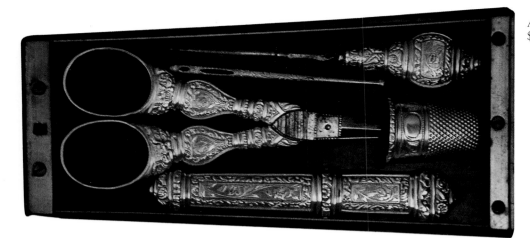

A French, 18 ct. gold set, c. 1830.
$1360/£850.

An 18 ct. gold set, c. 1840.
$1360/£850.

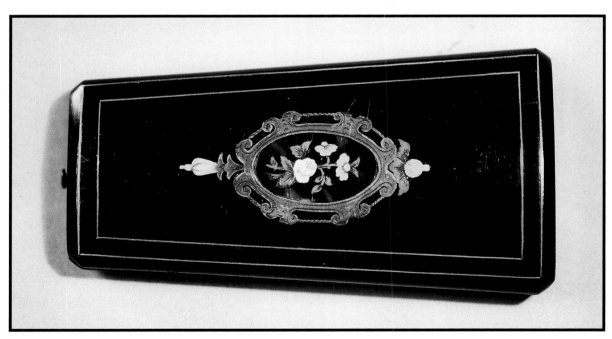

Exterior of the 18 ct. gold set.

A hand-painted lacquer box.

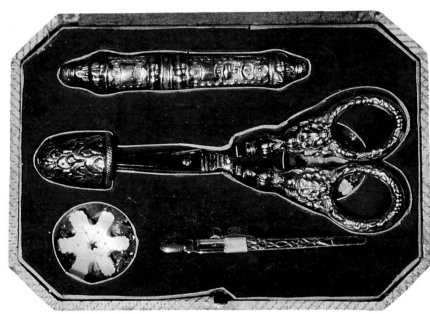

The tools inside, which are probably from Austria or Italy.

Left: an early, leather-type of Ladies Companion, with four leather cotton reel holders in the bottom. $480/£300.
Right: an unusual example of another Ladies Companion in green lacquer with exotic birds. $640/£400.

Two Ladies Companions in tooled leather made to resemble books, both c. 1850. $560/£350 each.

Rare French set in leather with all-leather clad tools including thimble and scissors. $640/£400.

A similar leather set with steel fittings and a separate metal needle container and thimble in the shape of a flask. $240/£150.

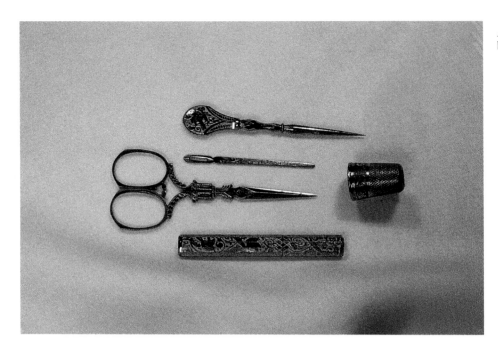

A set of steel and damascened tools, boxed in wood (box not shown).

Silver-plate fish étui, measuring 4" long. $560/£350.

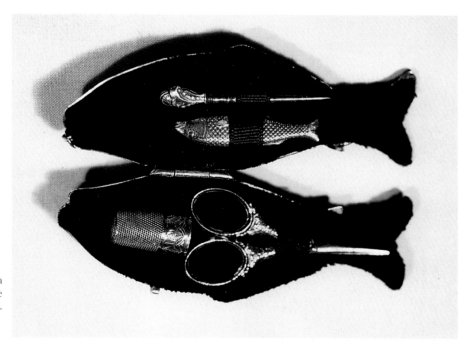

The fish étui opened to show a stiletto, a miniature "fish" needle case, thimble, and scissors.

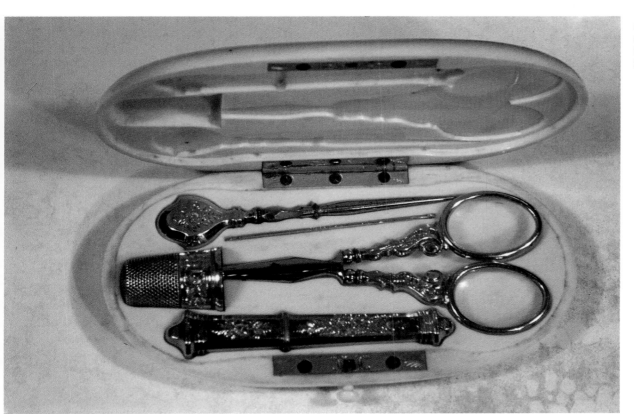

A typical French silver-gilt set in a fitted ivory box. $608/£380.

An Indian boxed set from Petragh, ivory and gold with gold filigree tools. $2,400/£1,500.

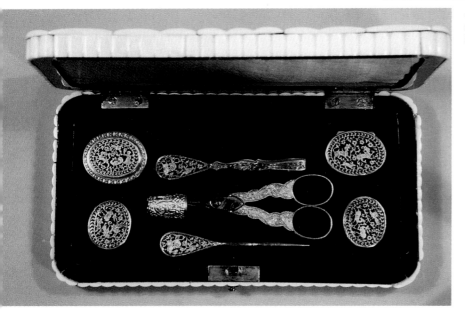

Miniature sewing sets, each just over 1" across, containing tiny tools.

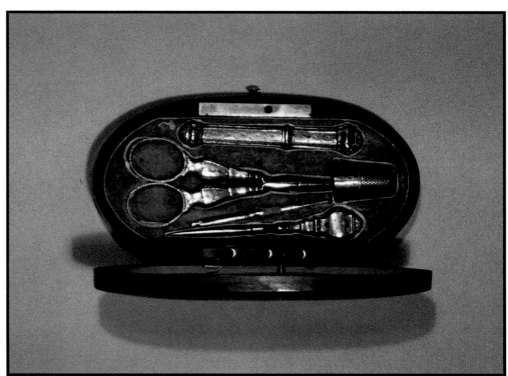

Tiny boxed set, 4" across, containing silver tools. $480/£300.

A miniature set in a tortoiseshell box, approximately 3.5" across. Shown with a Fern ware needle case, two leather pin cushions, and a metal acorn thread holder.

Two Spanish walnuts mounted in gilded metal, each containing a thimble, scissors, and stiletto. The lower one has a miniature book which gives advice on love (written in French). Both c. 1830. $960-1,120/£600-700 each.

Two tiny sets, approximately 1" across, inside nutshells. Both owned by Silvano Sorani of Italy.

Miniature ivory reel holder, approx. 4" high.

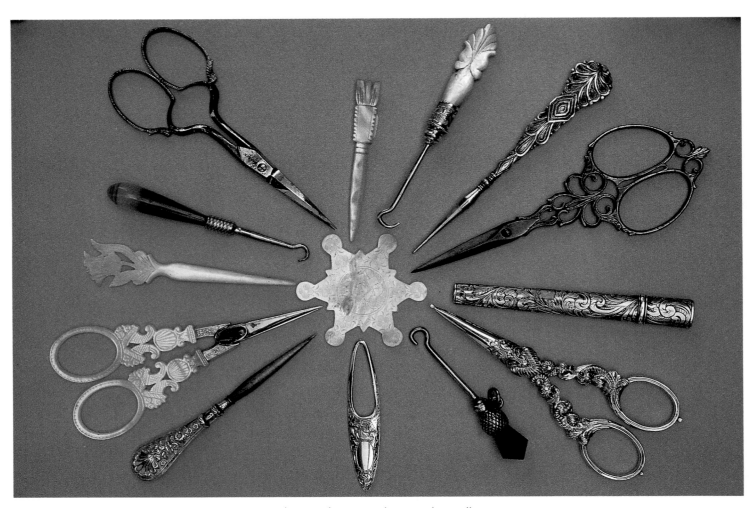

A selection of scissors, stilettos, and a needle case.

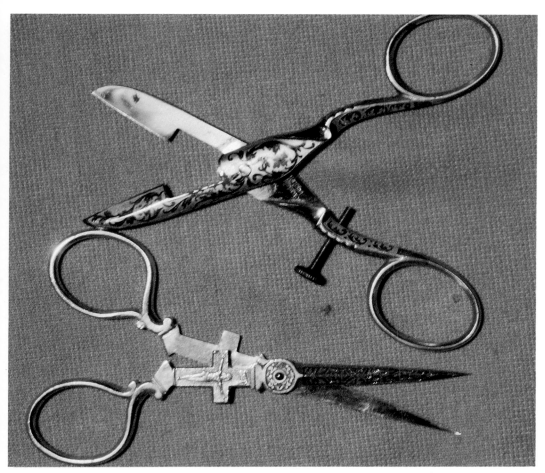

Two pairs of scissors, one in steel with a silver-gilt crucifix, probably made in Toledo as a religious souvenir, c. 1860. The other pair is decorated with Tula work and is for making button holes. The side screw can be adjusted according to the size of the hole required.

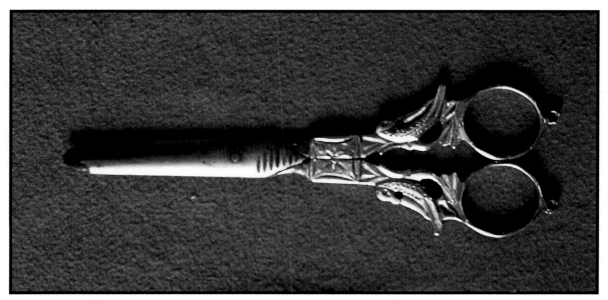

A pair of steel-bladed, silver-handled scissors, Dutch, c. 1810. Note the typically longer blades.

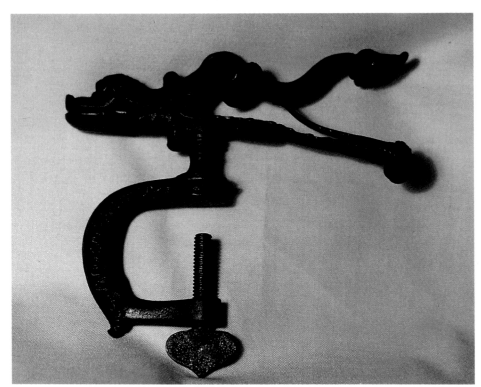

Iron clamp showing a mythical
dolphin, early nineteenth century.
$480/£300.

A steel clamp, mid-nineteenth
century. $240/£150.

A wooden clamp with unusual finial of a dog's head. $240/£150.

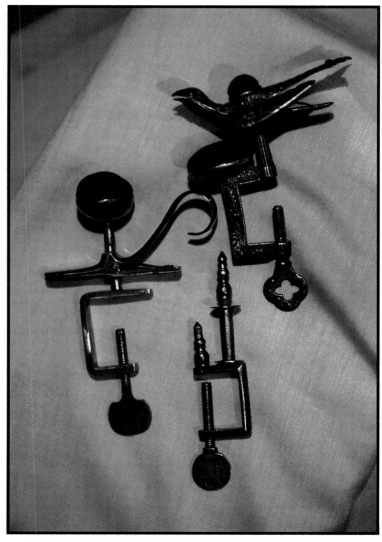

A Hemming bird clamp, followed by two other metal clamps, mid-nineteenth century. $288/£180, $192/£120, and $136/£85.

Selection of nineteenth century
novelty thimble holders. $96/
£60 plus each.

Selection of nineteenth century Mauchlin
and two metal thimble holders. $96/£60
plus each.

Above: Selection of various thimble holders, including the very popular little glass shoes made in various colors during the mid-nineteenth century.

Below: Nineteenth century novelty thimble holders, some in the shape of animals. The heads of the two in the back row lift off to reveal the thimble. In the front row, the iron is a novelty tape-measure and the donkey is pulling a cotton reel. $128-320/£80-200.

Selection of nineteenth century shoes. Some are pin cushions and some are thimble holders. $80-160/£50-100.

An exotic peacock in metal whose tail lifts up to reveal a cavity for a thimble, pecking at a pin cushion. $240/£150.

Novelty thimble cases including a rare alabaster case from Colwyn Bay in Wales,
a dog's head, and a pair of binoculars for a pair of thimbles. $128-320/£80-200.

A further selection: the parrot on the bakelite hussif is c. 1930, to the right is a rare butterfly in metal with the thimble cavity between its wings. Values from $80-160/£50-100, with the butterfly at over $160/£100.

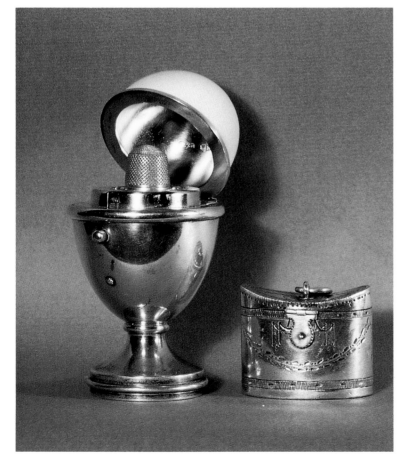

Novelty silver and ivory thimble, needle, and pin holder, with a provenance suggesting that it was given as a present to Princess Alexandra, wife of Edward VII. $800/£500.

Novelty silver case in the form of a fir cone with matching silver thimble decorated with fir cones. No hallmarks. $720/£450.

Three silver thimble holders. Left: a typical American example, shaped like a cylindrical box with a central post inside. Middle: Continental. Right: English, c. 1880. $320/£200 plus each.

Three brass reel holders. The one on the left has finials shaped like acanthus buds and two swimming pelicans, the one in the center has cherub finials with a tiny bird on each outstretched hand. *Courtesy of Rita Heath.*

A brass holder with ivory finials.
Courtesy of Rita Heath.

A wooden holder.
Courtesy of Rita Heath.

Left: a horizontal stand. Right: a rare example with a cockatoo whose head tilts back on a hinge to house a brass thimble. *Courtesy of Rita Heath.*

Three wooden holders. From left: rosewood, mixed woods, William IV in rosewood. *Courtesy of Rita Heath.*

Styles, Fashions, and Techniques used to Decorate Tools

Although boxes and châtelaines were fashionable, many separate sewing tools were made for the middle class market. There was an ever growing demand for goods in the medium price range for financially comfortably merchants' wives, who might want to show off their delicate embroidery in the drawing rooms of their new suburban villas. Tools were made in a variety of wares and materials coming from many parts of the Empire, and of course there were swings in fashion influenced by current affairs. The middle class Victorian woman was spoilt for choice.

There was a constant demand for commemorative and souvenir items. Some articles are easily identifiable, often dated and illustrated. Others, which were made in the fashion following an important event, need extra help. An historical chronology has been provided at the back of this book, which may assist in identification. For example, elephants appeared on needle cases, such as those from Avery, when Queen Victoria became Empress of India in 1876. Egyptian motifs were featured when the first tombs were excavated and the artifacts put on display. The designs for the Great Exhibition are already well known to us, but there may be other events that are less familiar now.

Very rare elephant needle case made by Avery. The needle packets were put in the metal howdah on its back. $640/£400.

The development of the international trade fair—a primarily nineteenth century phenomenon—resulted in the display of goods, including sewing tools, from all over the globe. These huge exhibitions were held regularly throughout the years in many locations, a significant proportion of them in France, but others in Great Britain, the United States, Australia and elsewhere. Local craftsmen would have been exposed to, and no doubt inspired by, the styles and fashions of the fine works on display, sewing accessories among them. As a result, general standards of design and manufacture tended to rise, even at the lower end of the price scale. Items made of the most common materials, and by means of mass production, could be appealing and well-crafted. The English market was influenced and enriched by the best imported goods from East and West.

Cloisonné Work

The history of *Cloisonné* work goes back at least three thousand years, but the kind of sewing tools using this technique that you might find now would have been made in the nineteenth century and probably exhibited at a trade fair for the export market. Cloisonné work entails thin strips of metal being attached to a metal base to form cells not unlike a honeycomb. These cells are then filled with finely powdered glass, which is then fired at a high temperature until it fuses to the metal. When the enamel melts, it shrinks, so the process has to be repeated several times until the surface is level with the metal cells (cloisons). Finally the surface is polished to achieve a sheen.

One of the most difficult effects to achieve is shaded color within the same cloison. This effect is the sign of a very high quality piece; you can see it on the best Russian cloisonné thimbles, a pale rose shading into a dark rose red looking very delicate and life-like. In auction room catalogues, the technique of Russian cloisonné work is referred to as "Russian traditional style."

The Japanese used the cloisonné technique in the seventeenth century, but so far no early cloisonné sewing tools have been discovered. Chinese cloisonné was at its best in the eighteenth century, and some cloisonné sewing tools from that era have been seen. There was a further revival in Japan in the early nineteenth century, which is likely to be the most available current source. Russian cloisonné work is most evident on thimbles, mainly from the late nineteenth century and early twentieth, with perhaps the finest from before the Revolution.

The name Spa ware comes from a town in Belgium called Spa, which became famous for its curative waters. Henceforth, other towns in Europe having curative waters, such as Bath, were known as spas. Spa ware is easy to recognize because it nearly always has a painted floral motif decorating a wooden surface. Typical items to be found in Spa ware would be needle-books, round flat pin cushions, and tape-measures.

An example of Spa Ware showing the characteristic painted floral decoration.
Courtesy of Gillian Prtichard.

Japan Ware and Papier Mâché

Japanese lacquer ware was the best: no other Asian lacquer was considered so fine, smooth, and amazingly resilient. It was originally brought over in the eighteenth century, when it was decorated with landscape scenes and figures in gold. Then, because of its popularity and cost, it was copied in England. There was a revival of imitation English Japan ware in the mid nineteenth century. The English imitators used a black varnish applied to a cheap wooden carcass. The article, perhaps a sewing box, achieved an ebonized, or lacquered, finish and might then be decorated with gold figures.

Another technique used to imitate Japanese lacquer was *papier mâché*, itself a French term! Henry Clay of Birmingham had patented papier mâché panels in 1772. The firm of Jennens & Bettridge took out a patent in 1825, and a further one in 1847, to ornament papier mâché with pearl shell and to soften it with steam in order to mould it into furniture, boxes, and sewing tables. Artists were employed to paint all manner of patterns and scenes, and they would tint the shell and gild the borders. If you are lucky, you might find a box with the Jennens & Bettridge label.

Bead Work

Bead work has always been popular. It is such a pretty, cheap way to transform a simple bone needle or thimble case. In the early nineteenth century, a fine net would be made, using your netting set, and beads threaded onto it using a tiny needle. The finest bead work came from France and was known as sable work, *sable* meaning sand. It is possible to collect beaded articles—such as card cases, boxes of all shapes and sizes, pin cushions, and scissors sheaths—

Three items in the very fine sable beadwork. The photo is indistinct but does show examples of good condition card cases and needle cases in this rare work, with original bright colors. Approximately $480/£300 each.

even now. The problem is finding them in good condition. You can often find little purses, waiting to be finished, at the bottom of a work box; they are always a colorful delight. Don't hesitate to buy damaged articles cheaply in order to salvage the beads, as it is possible to find repairers but *not* possible to buy the very fine beads now, even in specialist shops. As of this writing, there is a trimmings stand in the Portobello Road, London, where you can buy old material and trimmings for repairs, as you may need to reline a bead work purse. Tiny beads are often found in little wooden containers in old sewing boxes, so do not throw them away.

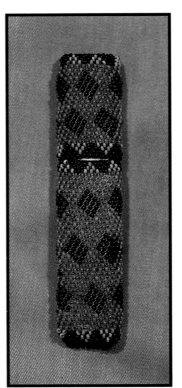

Bead covered bone needle case, English, c. 1860. $96/£60.

Detail of a further example of sable work on a card case.

Mauchlin Ware

The Mauchlin ware industry was started by two brothers, William and Andrew Smith of Mauchlin in Ayrshire, Scotland. They began in the early 1820s, making all sorts of souvenir objects out of sycamore and birch. Early examples had scenes of well known beauty spots and monuments painted directly onto the wood, which was then varnished. Many of these early scenes would have been views that were familiar to the Scottish poet Robert Burns, who was raised in Mauchlin. As the Smith brothers' business grew, they had to find a quicker method of decoration; by the 1840s, the scenes were first painted onto oval or square pieces of paper, then glued to the wood and varnished. The next step was to put a transfer print straight onto the wood. These souvenirs were bought by tourists visiting Scotland, and were made in quantity. The brothers expanded into making foreign souvenirs for export, which is why American and continental scenes appear in the mid-nineteenth century. In the 1890s, monochrome photos replaced the transfer prints. There is a Mauchlin Society which is always researching new information, especially regarding the identification of scenes from abroad.[3]

Selection of Mauchlin ware. Top, from left: a bottle thimble holder, a book needle case, and a thimble case. Bottom: three pin cushions. $64-96/£40-60 each.

A paper-covered, round string holder, a Mauchlin clamp with a rare print of Covent Garden Opera House, a cylindrical knitting-needle case, a small cylindrical needle case, and another paper-covered string holder.

Top: a Mauchlin pin wheel and two thimble cases. Bottom: a needle book and two pin cushions. $64-96/£40-60 each.

Close up of the Mauchlin needle book.

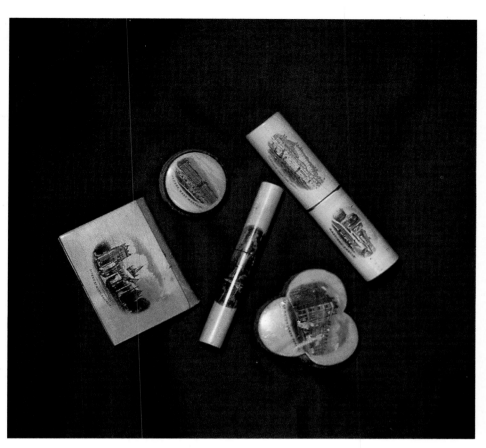

Selection of Mauchlin ware: a needle book, two pin cushions, and two cylindrical needle cases. $64-96/£40-60 each.

Fern Ware

Fern ware is a similar process to Mauchlin ware, but it was started in the 1880s. The decoration is of ferns and sometimes seaweed and shells. The early pieces look more like fossilized prints of ferns. This look was achieved by using a real fern as a stencil, spraying paint around it. When the leaf was removed, it left a ghost-like print. Seaweed was also used in a similar fashion. Later pieces had groups of shells and seaweed printed on them.

A group of three Fern ware pin wheels. $56/£35 each.

Tartan Ware

Tartan ware is probably the most prized out of the three forms of Mauchlin ware. This is because it has a big following in the United States, perhaps due to people interested in finding the tartan of one of their forebears. The tartan paper was first printed in sheets (using many of the popular tartans), cut up and glued to the wooden carcass, and finally varnished against scratches. The seams were cleverly hidden by black strips printed with gilt lines. Hand-painted scenes were featured on the early pieces, but monochrome photos were used on some later items.

Two examples of Mauchlin Tartan ware: a needle book and a cylindrical needle case. Approximately $128/£80 each.

Assortment of Tartan ware items. From left: a string holder (paper-covered, not tartan), a notebook, a Tartan reel holder box, a spectacle case, a stamp box, and a book. $192-320/£120-200.

More Tartan ware. From left: a combination tape-measure and cotton holder, a pin cushion in front of a pin wheel, a tulip vase to hold spills, a cotton winder, a go-to-bed (which held wax matches with which you lit the way to bed by putting one in the little ivory finial at the top), a cylindrical needle case, a reel holder box with two photographic portraits, another spill vase, another cotton reel holder box with a photographic portrait. In front of the boxes: a pin cushion and emery, a paper knife, a shuttle and tape-measure, a pen wiper (to wipe your pen nibs on), and another winder.

Straw-work

Straw-work dates from the late eighteenth century and was in vogue well into the nineteenth. During that period, wages were relatively low and the cost of materials, such as precious metals, was high. Straw was virtually free, often gleaned after the harvest. Children were employed to comb and dye it, then it was formed into patterns and stuck onto cheap wooden carcasses. The patterns and scenes were amazingly intricate and the colors bright, giving the whole object a certain lightness and gaiety.

Straw-work is sometimes referred to as "prisoner of war work," although much of it looks far too professional for the work of poor imprisoned French soldiers. There was a prison at Norman Cross, which was the source of many of the fine exhibits of prisoner of war work now on view in the Peterborough Museum. As well as straw, prisoners fashioned articles out of bone, which they carved and painted. Prisoners taken during the wars with France were expected to work for their keep. The money they earned from goods sold from their stalls in the prison yard was taken to pay for food, otherwise they starved. British soldiers and sailors did not fare much better abroad; they wandered about Europe, also making and selling what they could in order to get home—so prisoner of war work is not an English phenomenon. Europe was still recovering from a period of warfare, thus goods and sewing tools made at that time reflect a lack of expensive materials coupled with an abundance of skilled labour.

Straw-work items. Top to bottom: a case for needles, bodkins, or netting tools; a silk-lined egg-shaped thimble case with a draw-string pouch and another egg thimble holder; needle holders on either side of what are possibly card cases; two long flat holders for silk skeins used in embroidery. *Exhibit from the Peterborough Museum of Prisoner of War Work, photographed by Peter Moyse A.R.P.S. of Peterborough.*

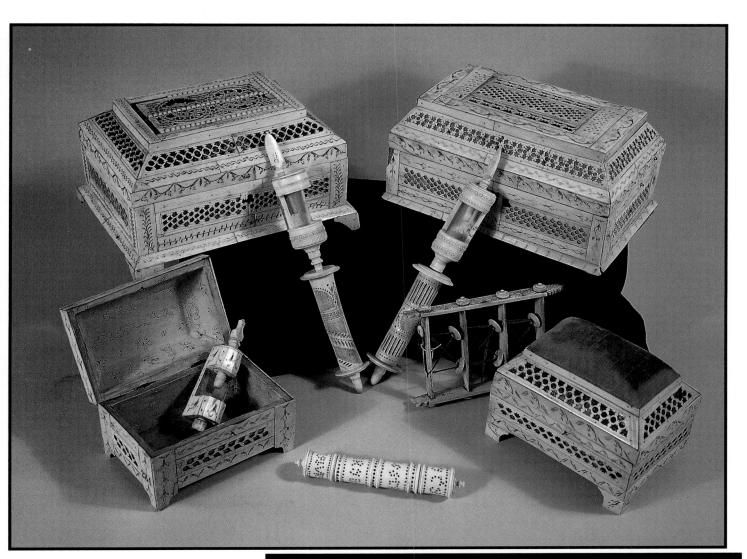

A selection of bone and ivory boxes for sewing and trinkets. The smaller two boxes in the front have pin cushions tops. There are two fine clamps with fretwork, or pierced work, holders for needles, a smaller clamp on the left, and a bodkin or crochet hook case at the bottom. No one is sure what the ladder construction on the right was used for. *Exhibit from the Peterborough Museum of Prisoner of War Work, photographed by Peter Moyse A.R.P.S. of Peterborough.*

A shoal of little fish winders with slits in their mouths and tails for holding thread. Shown with two exquisite cut-out work trinket baskets. *Exhibit from the Peterborough Museum of Prisoner of War Work, photographed by Peter Moyse A.R.P.S. of Peterborough.*

Painted Tunbridge Ware and Tunbridge Stick Ware

A mechanical construction of wheels and platforms measuring 3.5" high, enclosed in a glass case, possibly used in prisoner of war work.

Tunbridge ware is another example of an inexpensive material used to great advantage. At the end of the eighteenth century, there was a small town in Kent called Tunbridge Wells, which was known for the curative properties of its drinking wells. During the Great Plague of London many people fled to Tunbridge to escape the mortal illness and take the waters. It is said that the little town had no lodgings in the seventeenth century and even Queen Henrietta-Maria and her entourage had to sleep in tents. Soon the townsfolk began to realize the commercial potential of the waters, and houses were built to lodge visiting aristocracy. As visitors arrived in ever greater numbers, shops opened to sell local souvenirs. By the nineteenth century the town was thriving and fashionable. A local woodturner called Wise, who had previously made trenchers and wooden dishes, expanded his business into making boxes using local woods; these included yew, holly, furze, and imported lignum vitae. Tunbridge became famous for high quality veneer and inlaid wood called marquetry or *marquette*. The green wood, limb-wood, grew in small quantities, and was only used on better quality early sewing boxes and tools. The painted ware, made at the end of the eighteenth century until c.1830, was cheaper to make than inlay, but never as popular. Typical examples of sewing tools in painted ware had circles of green, red, and yellow on plain beech.

A selection of thimble cases, three in painted Tunbridge and the bottom left in stick Tunbridge ware. Each approximately $320/£200. In the center, a wooden thimble.

Stick ware, or end-grain mosaic, came in after painted ware, and was an attempt to lower the high cost of *marquette* work. To make end-grain mosaic, narrow strips of hardwood are glued together, then sliced through and applied like a veneer. The most comprehensive book on Tunbridge ware, by the late Edward Pinto, suggests that you can date by design. Marquetry cubes (also known as the tumbling box design) date from the eighteenth century, but when accompanied by end-grain mosaic they date from the late 1820s. But-terflies and birds were featured from the 1820s to the 1850s. According to Gay Ann Rogers, the floral designs were borrowed from Berlin wool work patterns for embroidery (up until the 1870s), as Berlin work was the trend-setting craze of the middle class. Today's collector can find delightful tape-measures, waxers, clamps, and thimble cases in stick ware. Painted ware items might include clamps, tape-measures, and thimble cases.

An early painted Tunbridge ware sewing box made as a miniature house, a Tunbridge stick ware sewing clamp, and an eighteenth century embroidered picture of Diana the Huntress.

A selection of painted Tunbridge tools taken from a box: reel holders, a tape-measure, and a thimble case. On the right is an example of Spa work (described earlier in this chapter), a needle case in wood with painted flowers.

A painted Tunbridge ware clamp.$320/£200.

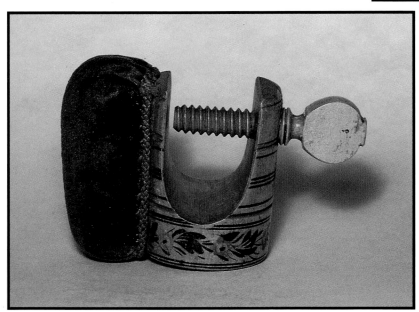

The same clamp, showing the velvet cushion at the top for pins.

An assortment of tools: a stick ware Tunbridge thimble case; a tape-measure in ebony with an ivory crown finial; a bakelite bear tape-measure; a combination Tunbridge ware tape-measure, waxer, and pin cushion.

A Tunbridge stick ware thimble, known as the most expensive little bit of wood in the world, as it fetched approximately $480/£300 at auction.

A selection of Tunbridge stick ware: a needle box, winder case, waxer and pin cushion, and pin wheel.

Ivory and its Embellishments

Tools made from wood, bone, and straw are most attractive, but to some they lack the air of luxury that ivory can provide. Ivory was still extremely popular for tools; it was glossier and less grainy than the bone used by prisoners of war, and not too expensive due to Britain's continuing imports from India. Various forms of embellishments were used to decorate it: these included hot needle work, known as *Madras,* hailing originally from India; and *Clouté* work from France (pronounced *clue-tay*), which is the use of tiny nails hammered into the ivory—watch out for signs of rust from the pre-stainless steel pins or nails bleeding into the surrounding ivory. *Shibayama* decoration, originating in Japan, is typically of tiny insects and flowers inlaid with mother-of-pearl, stained ivory, coral, and horn. Tortoiseshell is used to make the small branches, coconut shell employed for the tree trunks.

Shibayama work on sewing tools is very rare, but sewing boxes can be found, with the tools inside made of silver. Some shibayama boxes are made from halves of tusks, hinged and placed on little bun feet. Never wash ivory, as this dries it, removes the sheen, and causes any embellishments to run or discolor. If it has gone yellow or stained, take it to an ivory restorer to bleach professionally; don't waste time with lemon juice and home remedies as they can make the problem worse.

Selection of ivory tools. Middle row, left to right: a waxer, a needle case decorated with Madras work in red and black, a glove hook, a pin wheel decorated with Madras work and initial C in center, a stiletto, and a needle case. At the back is a small box, in the front a tambour hook, a Cantonese-work needle case, and a plain thimble.

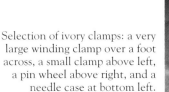

Selection of ivory clamps: a very large winding clamp over a foot across, a small clamp above left, a pin wheel above right, and a needle case at bottom left.

One of the famous fisher-folk needle cases showing a fisherwoman opening at the waist to reveal a cylinder for needles, early nineteenth century, probably made in Dieppe as a souvenir and one of a pair.

Ivory and gold mounted pin poppet, c. 1820. $400/£250.

A pair of fisher-folk, a man and a woman. $800/£500 for pair.

Selection of tools. Top row: a tambour hook with steel butterfly screw. Next row: a gold studded ivory scent bottle container; a carved ivory tape, an eighteenth century thimble case, and a mother-of-pearl needle case. Next row: a silver tape-measure at far left and an acorn-shaped ivory tape-measure. Next row: a silver needle case, a fine Dieppe work notebook carved with a bunch of grapes, an eighteenth century sewing étui, a French silver needle case, and an ivory needle case in the shape of a fish. Bottom row: a rare mother-of-pearl needle case.

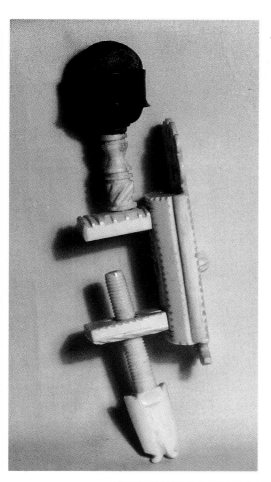

An ivory clamp, c.
1830. $240/£150.

Above, right and below:
Rare Shibyama needle
book. Front view, back
view, and inside showing
little ivory winders and
needle packet.

Front view of the
clamp above.

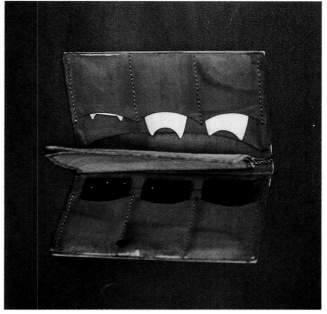

Selection of tools. Left to right: an ivory tambour hook; a pierced wax holder or pomander; a tall double emery and pin cushion with a tape-measure at the top in painted ware; two examples of cut-out fretwork pin cushions c. 1830, a wheelbarrow and a sledge; a vegetable ivory cut-out pomander.

Two ivory needle cases, a key inlaid with steel and a Chinaman finely carved in an early nineteenth century manner.

Possibly late eighteenth or early nineteenth century finely carved ivory needle case with a central opening, possibly from Dieppe.

Late eighteenth century ivory thimble holder with thimble. The column in the lid opens to take needles, probably French.

Ivory and gilt thimble holder and needle case, c. 1830.

A painted ivory thimble, probably French, c. 1820.

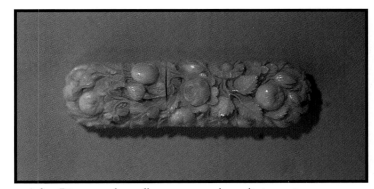

A fine Dieppe work needle case—note the realistic carving.

Cantonese ivory work is recognizable by the deeply carved figures in a Chinese landscape. This work came from the port of Canton during the early nineteenth century. Although much of our ivory, and many ivory tools, came from India, the opinion amongst the cognoscenti is that Chinese exports in general reached a far higher standard of refinement. On the other hand, there were more British women in India and therefore a bigger market to please and sell sewing things to, as well as more women on the spot to explain the desired requirements. As is the case with some tools made for export, their use was not fully understood. The Chinese ivory shuttles, for example, although lovely to look at, seem too flat to function well.

A group of Cantonese sewing tools. Top right: a needle case and below it an expandable needle case. Left: a clamp and another needle case, then a flat shuttle, the type that seems too flat to use. Some of these items have been lent by Elena Innocenti of ARCA in Gray's Antiques, London.

Pierced work, sometimes called *fretwork,* was mainly done in Europe. It is the name given to ivory tools that have a pierced decoration, which produces a light, airy look. The effect achieved looks like ivory lace. This work was used particularly on winders, where whole scenes were pierced out on a small surface. The finest fretwork was produced in the eighteenth century, often with figures, such as cupids, interspersed amongst the fretting. Thimble cases and bod-

kin holders are two items you might find. The problem is that once it is damaged, which occurs easily, it is nearly impossible to repair. *Piqué* decoration is also extremely fine; it is made by inlaying tiny pieces of silver, and sometimes gold, to form delicate designs. It was often used on tortoiseshell as well as ivory and mother-of-pearl.

A selection of tools, mainly in cut-out fretwork. Left to right: a combination tape-measure and pin wheel, a small pin cushion, a larger combination pin cushion and tape-measure, separate tape-measure decorated with Madras or hot needle work, a double-ended pin cushion and emery; a novelty tape.

Vegetable Ivory

If you could not afford ivory, the next best thing was vegetable ivory, a material in which a great quantity of sewing tools were made. The name vegetable ivory was used to describe both the corozo and the coquilla nut, as both were used as cheap substitutes for ivory. The coquilla nut is the darker of the two, and the one most likely to have been used for items made in the seventeenth and eighteenth as well as the nineteenth centuries. The coquilla was used to make late seventeenth century pomanders, often carved in extraordinary detail. Later, carved and pierced eggs, which unscrew in the middle, were made to hold scented wax. Tiny scented wax holders or pomanders are sometimes found in sewing boxes. You can identify them by the pierced holes which let the scent through.

The corozo has a waxy finish, and is creamy/brown in color, often with small brown dots or blotches. The usable parts of both nuts are small, so only small items could be made, or items that were made in several sections. The tools are often charming, but the carving on the corozo rarely achieves the depth and skill of execution found on ivory. Any painted decoration tends to wear off completely, owing to the ultra smooth, non-porous surface. The most common tools made were tape-measures, acorn-shaped thimble cases, and pin cushions.

Selection of ivory and vegetable ivory thimbles. The middle thimble in the bottom row is vegetable ivory (note the browner color and waxy finish), the other thimbles are ivory.

Gold Sewing Tools

As the merchant classes grew in prosperity, there was, of course, a booming market for gold and gem set tools and sets. A disproportionate number of those remain to us, perhaps because they would have been well looked after. As hallmarking small items in gold or silver was not obligatory until the late nineteenth century, many good quality items are not marked. Below is a guide, however, that may be of some use to collectors.

Gold sewing tools are not, in the main, hallmarked, so it is not very easy to ascertain the gold content, i.e., their carat. In general, however, Victorian tools were made in 15-carat gold, with 9-carat examples appearing in the late nineteenth century through to the beginning of the twentieth. The basic guideline to follow is that the heavier the gold, the higher the carat (though there are always exceptions).

In the nineteenth century, France and Switzerland generally used 18-carat gold (lower carats were not recognized as gold there), Great Britain used 9, 15, and 18, while the United States preferred 14, and occasionally 18. German gold is accepted as low as 8-carat, but such pieces are more often of twentieth century vintage.

Amazingly, there are forty-eight registered colors of gold (although you cannot discern the carat of gold by its color). The most common varieties are white gold (gold mixed with silver), rose gold (gold mixed with copper), green gold (gold mixed with various alloys), and pure gold, which is 24-carat and somewhat rare due to its impractical soft state.

If a piece of gold does not have a hallmark (that is, carat mark), a professional jeweler can use the so-called acid test to ascertain exactly what the carat of the gold is or whether the article is merely gold-plated.

Instead of a hallmark, so-called convention marks often appear: 18-carat gold is marked "750," 14-carat "585." and 9-carat "375." On imported goods, 22-carat gold is stamped "916," 18-carat "750," 14-carat "585," and 9-carat "375." Over the years, British gold standards have been lowered: up to 1798, 22-carat was the standard; from 1798-1854, 22- and 18-carat; from 1854-1931, 9-, 12-, and 15-carat; and since 1931, 9-, 12-, and 14-carat.

Hallmarks on French sewing tools are often difficult to decipher but, if clear, the following may help:

1809-1819	Cock's head	Paris gold
1819-1838	Cock	gold and silver
	Rabbit's head	Paris silver
After 1838	Eagle's head	Paris gold
	Horse's head	Provinces' gold
	Boar's head	Paris silver
	Crab	Provinces' silver

An owl identifies objects otherwise unmarked from 1838. French sewing tools are becoming more appreciated now, owing to their beauty of design. If you have perseverance, and a lot of time to spare, buy Tardy's book on *Foreign Gold and Silver Hallmarks*. It is fiendishly difficult to follow, but it can be useful.

A selection of gold, jeweled and enamel thimbles from the nineteenth century. Each thimble $640+/£400+

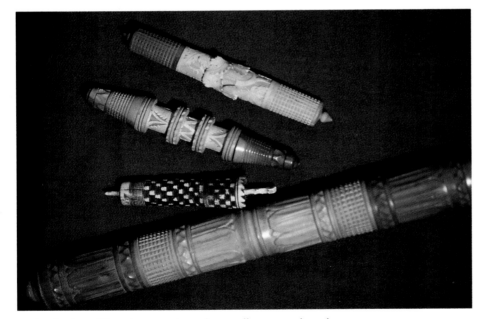

A selection of Bavarian carved wooden needle cases and one larger knitting needle case. $48-80/£30-50

Austrian and German Sewing Tools

Within the overall field of sewing tools, there are so many areas to potentially specialize in. Sewing is universal, so you have every country in the world to choose from. It may help to know some identifying details of tools from various places.

Nineteenth century tools made in both Austria and Germany were often attractive silver examples with embossed decoration. Many of these were unmarked, but those that *were* marked might include a number indicating the "Loth," i.e., the standard unit of silver purity in Austria, Germany, and much of central Europe. The numbers 12 and 13 represented .725 and .825 respectively. This system of marking was discontinued around 1860. The silver weight is inclined to feel lighter, in general, than an equivalent English article. Other distinctive tools were wood carved, often using a motif of grapes, on perhaps a bodkin or knitting needle case. Tiny carved horn goats' feet were often made as knitting needle protectors.

Russian Sewing Tools

Not all Russian silver and gold sewing tools were hallmarked, but if they were, the hallmark was either "84" or "88." Until 1925, the "Slothnik" was the Russian unit of purity applied to silver, with "96" representing pure silver. From 1896-1907, a woman's head facing left was sometimes used on silver, and from 1908-1917 a woman's head facing right, but such marks are rare. After 1927, the "84" changed to "88" or ".875." The more marks on a piece of silver, the more important that piece, so four marks—for instance "84," the factory name, the town where it was made, and the maker's initial—denote a significant piece of silver. The number "56" found on gold pieces denotes the mark for St. Petersburg.

The Russian tools you are most likely to find now are the famous Russian enamel thimbles. Needle cases do turn up very occasionally, and I once saw a Russian silver and enamel châtelaine in an auction. Russian sewing boxes have not found their way here yet, but the odd silver boxed set has been spotted. If you have the luck to see anything Russian, having looked at the quality, take a chance because these items are very rare.

End of an Era

On 20th June 1897, Queen Victoria's Diamond Jubilee was celebrated by a vast crowd outside St. Paul's Cathedral. The Grandmother of Europe, as she was popularly known, was moved and gratified. Britain was stable and prosperous, and on the whole conservative in taste and spirit. The conditions for our poor seamstresses were now somewhat better, although life was still hard and wages for women low. Victorian taste in all areas, including sewing tools, reflected a desire for solid middle class values, of quality without ostentation. The materials used were the best and things were built to last, the Dorcas thimble being a good example. However, with the ever growing popularity and availability of the sewing machine, hand sewing and its accompanying tools were on the decline.

Assorted Tools from the Nineteenth Century

A group of tools. At the back, an egg thimble holder, a Tunbridge combination tape-measure and thimble holder, a miniature sewing set in a metal globe, and a painted notebook. In the front, a Fern ware emery and pin cushion and a similar in Tartan ware. $96-160/£60-100 each.

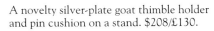
A novelty silver-plate goat thimble holder and pin cushion on a stand. $208/£130.

A selection of winders in wood, bone, and mother-of-pearl with two rare Tunbridge examples in the center.

From left: a bear pin cushion and thimble holder. $128/£80; a cockerel pin holder. $128/£80; a pig tape-measure. $96/£60; and a squirrel tape-measure. $192/£120.

Selection of thimbles and ivory cotton reel holders.

Selection of thimble holders in
metal, silver and ivory.

A heavy glass mushroom-top slicker stone. A slicker stone, or linen smoother, was used to iron and glaze the linen with a circular sweeping movement, and was made of glass, marble, or lignum.

Two pin cushions and a thimble case.

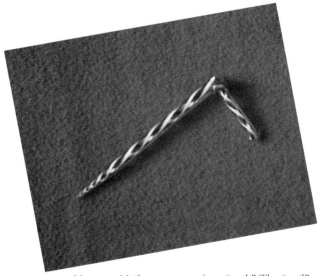

Very rare Nailsea measure for a "nail." The "nail" was an earlier form of measuring used, for example, on tape-measures before the inch came in. This little Nailsea novelty could be used to measure out a nail on your silk tape-measure, which you would then mark in yourself.

Selection of pin cushions. Colored prints of historical British scenes, under glass. Sometimes there is a mirror on the reverse. From $112/£70 each.

Two Nanny pin sets with gold stones, with inside needle compartment and cotton holder at the side. $96/£60 each.

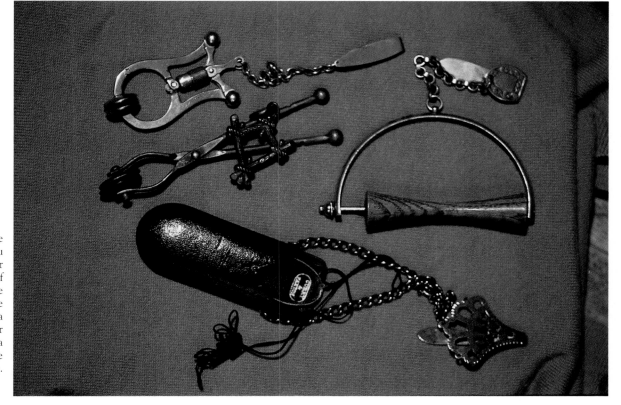

The top two items are skirt lifters in metal. You attached the hook to your belt and put the hem of your long skirt into the clip to keep it out of the mud. On the right, a working spool knave for thread. At the bottom, a leather spectacle case châtelaine.

Selection of novelty tape-measures: a soup tureen, a rugby ball, a coffee grinder, a spring loaded tape, and a rare silver kettle with an agate handle.

An assortment of metal tape-measures: a rare lawn mower, $240/£150; a coffee grinder, $96/£60; a tankard, $96/£60; and a thimble holder.

A rare silver shoe pin cushion set with Scottish hard stones, c. 1890.

More tape-measures. Back row: a vegetable ivory and bakelite ship. Second row: vegetable ivory and bakelite animal in a shoe. Bottom row: metal tapes including a clock where the hands revolve as you wind out the tape.

A very fine black work stitched picture and two nineteenth century embroidered bell pulls. Picture: approximately $480/£300. Bell pulls: approximately $128/£80 each.

A selection of Baxter print needle boxes, c. 1840. Baxter prints were some of the finest prints in detail, coloring, and representation used to decorate little boxes containing needle packets—the last sets being made in 1859. Their only rival was a French print maker called Le Blond who also decorated needle boxes with prints in a similar manner, c. 1850. Each of these boxes would fetch approximately $48/£30 in good condition.

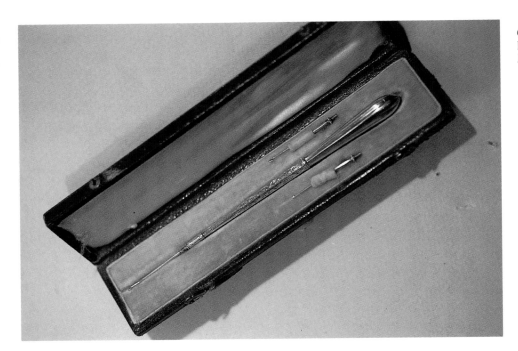

Gold crochet hook set with extra hooks. *Courtesy of Elena Innocenti.* $560/£350.

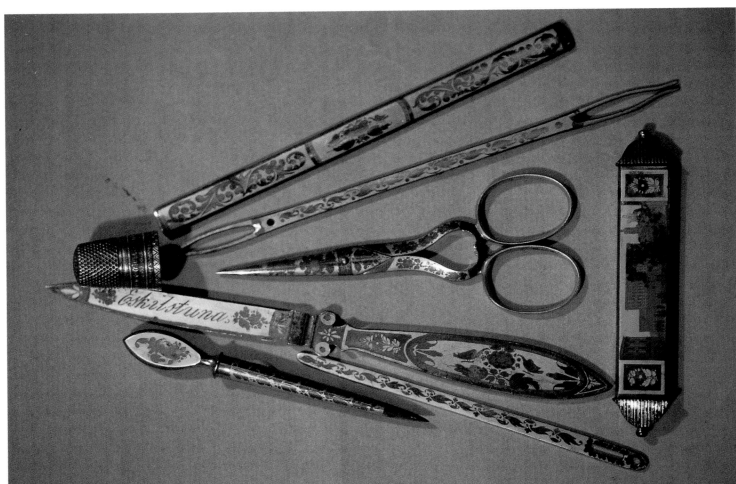

Selection of rare Tula work tools. Tula work is a form of gilded decoration on steel, originating from Russia, however this particular set comes from the north of Scandinavia. It is not unlike Toledo steel work.

Selection of needle cases.

A painted metal needle case—not made by Avery. Approximately $192/£120.

Novelty fish sewing sets in metal. The lower one with the red glass eye is a tape-measure. $160-800/£100-500 each.

Selection of wood and
ivory clamps.

Silver and mother-of-pearl
handled crotchet hook. *Courtesy
of Elena Innocenti.*

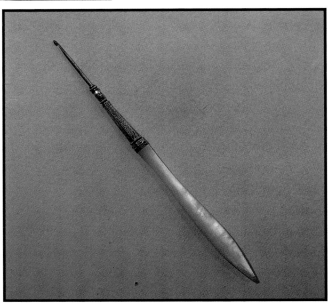

Three Avery needle cases.
$80-240/£50-150.

Very rare metal tureen needle case made by Avery.
$480/£300.

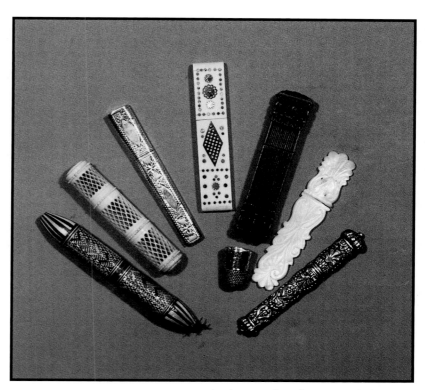

A selection of needle cases, including an
eighteenth century ivory case with steel
decoration in the center.

A winding swift for wool. $128/£80.

Chapter Six

The Twentieth Century

Prince Edward was fifty-nine when Queen Victoria died in 1901. The Edwardian era, though only nine years in length, was an age of intellectual advancement and brilliant achievements. The King loved travel and was keen to follow international developments on the Continent. He encouraged elegance of design and a love of beauty that had formerly been frowned upon by his mother. Just looking at the abundance of small, flat, leather boxed sets from this era gives one an awareness of the growing mobility in lifestyles. Trains, ships, bicycles, and cars were transporting people about in great numbers, so traveling sets became necessary. The rich, having servants to carry luggage, could have large combined sewing and toilet sets. These were beautifully fitted out with toilet bottles, toothbrushes, combs, and manicure items, as well as sewing tools. The less rich

had smaller flat leather boxed sets and, as the century progressed, even handbag-sized little kits.

Silver was used to a greater extent than it had been, partly due to its availability at a lower cost, and partly due to higher wages being paid. It was not cost effective to pay a good wage to a workman spending time on a cheap set or box that would not ultimately command the high price of silver. All manner of silver tools were made, as well as the ubiquitous small leather covered sets containing a thimble and scissors. American tools were finding a strong market and achieving their own identity. The style in Britain during the Edwardian era was predominantly Neo-classical, a revival of the late eighteenth century classicism made popular by designers such as John Adam.

Spring-loaded tape-measures took over from the hand-wound ones: they were flat round tapes with a tight spring and ranged in material from celluloid to silver, some having advertising products on them. These have become collectible items on their own. Perhaps the most popular mid-twentieth century tapes to collect are the plastic figural ones.[1] The comic invention of the subject matter is what makes these so appealing. It is important to check if the tape still works, because they are impossible to repair. If there are a few inches missing, go ahead with the purchase if you like the subject. Sometimes you may think that your tape has a big crack in it, but they were

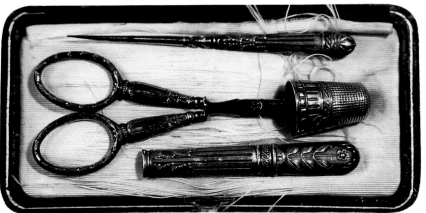

Turn-of-the-century French silver sewing set in the Edwardian Neo-classical style. $480/£300.

A selection of bakelite novelty tape-measures: a dog, boar, rabbit, elephant, and cockerel. All these bakelite tapes are now tremendously collectible, but it is important that they can be pulled out, even if not completely. $96-128/£60-80 each.

originally made in two pieces and then glued together, so do not be put off. A good example will cost you over $80 (£50) now.

Additional bakelite novelty tapes. Approximately $128/£80 each.

Detail of tape-measure with a bathing girl whose legs pull out. $160/£100.

Another tape-measure detail showing Charlie Chaplin's head. $144/£90.

Another selection of tape-measures.

Three metal novelty tapes: a champagne bottle, toucan and windmill. Approximately $128-288/£80-180 each.

A very rare metal tape of a performing bear. $240/£150.

Needle cases, tape-measure of a goblin, and a pin cushion.

During the 1920s, Art Deco was all the rage; the Jazz Age had arrived and its influence on all the decorative arts was clear. The 1920s planted the seeds of modern living, and mass-production played an increasing role in everyday life. The German equivalent of Art Deco was the *Jugendstil*. The designs were generally heavier than their French equivalents. They were rarely used on small sewing items, but occasionally evident on silver sets. The mass-production of aluminum (or, to give it its older name, alurine) meant that thimbles, hussifs, and threading devices were developed for advertising purposes and employed as giveaway tokens (Iles and Gomme were the dominant manufacturers).

Another immensely popular twentieth century collectible is the silver pin cushion. There was a particular vogue for animals, mostly made in the early and middle part of the century. Some collectors prefer only cushions with the original pads, but if they have been re-covered using old velvet that should not detract from the value. Most of them are hallmarked, but some marks are incomplete. With many sewing tools, owing to their size and relative unimportance, the hallmark was not always exact. Even the famous firm of Samson Mordan has a variety of incompleteness in their marking. Often you will find Rd 674398 (design registration number) and then a Chester mark but no letter, or maybe just Mordan without any assay mark or date letter.

A selection of English silver animal pin cushions, all c. 1910-1930. $320+/£200+ each.

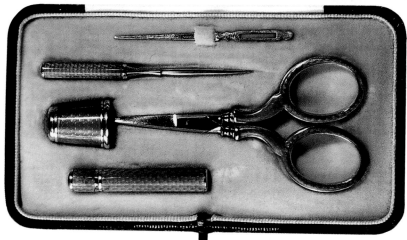

An early twentieth century silver and enamel sewing set, probably Scandinavian. The silver-gilt bodkin is not original. Approximately $480/£300.

Big box needle cases in cardboard are a very Edwardian phenomenon; they open out revealing all the needle packets. They often have pictures of famous beauties stuck onto the cardboard, very much to the Edwardian taste. The Art Nouveau style, with its celebration of curvaceous females, was a little too extravagant to be used on the small surfaces of sewing tools, the exception being one or two French sets and some American tools, including thimbles. The *femme fleur* (the woman as flower) was a popular motif, and was used on an American thimble made by Stern Bros. in c.1900. Cupid, the messenger of love, was another popular motif to be found on thimbles, crochet hooks, needle cases, card cases, and scent bottles. The original painting that inspired many of the designs is by Joshua Reynolds in the National Gallery.

A rare French commemorative sewing set with scissors and thimble made to celebrate the end of the First World War. The thimble on its own was known as *Le De de la Guerre*. $1,120/£700.

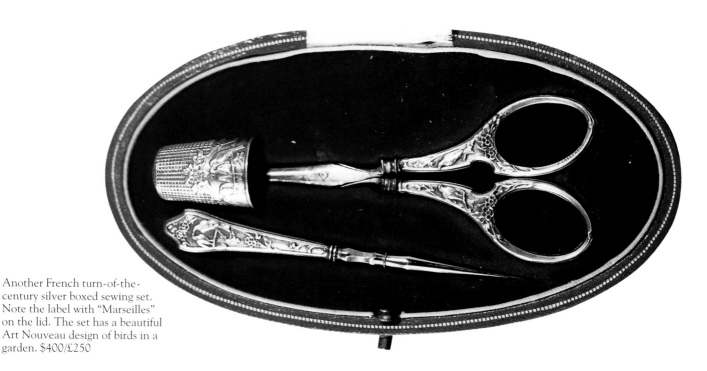

Another French turn-of-the-century silver boxed sewing set. Note the label with "Marseilles" on the lid. The set has a beautiful Art Nouveau design of birds in a garden. $400/£250

Decorative French Art Nouveau thimble.

Plastic handbag hussifs are very good fun; they were often made as little novelty dolls with cute black painted hair in a flapper style. The metal metrailleuse (pop out) needle cases with advertisements on them are again too common at the moment to warrant much attention. Nanny brooches, which were made out of brass with a central, often gold, stone, are much sought after. They have a central bar which holds needles and thread and unscrews at the end. They are not worth buying if the central thread holder is missing. They were worn by nannies so that they could carry out repairs to their charges' clothes on the spot. As the century progressed, hand-sewing became a thing of the past, or just a luxury pastime, so fewer tools were made. Commemorative thimbles are probably the best bet for investing in now.

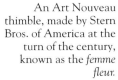
An Art Nouveau thimble, made by Stern Bros. of America at the turn of the century, known as the *femme fleur*.

To sum up twentieth century European tools, look for plastic figural tapes, silver pin cushions, and silver thimbles, especially the lovely Art Nouveau French and American ones. Elaborate silver châtelaines enjoyed yet another revival at the beginning of the century, and are very collectible. Always buy any separate pendant pieces which you can then add onto an incomplete châtelaine. Don't worry if all the pieces do not match; clips were often sold separately and people added what they required. This is especially true of continental examples. Silver needle cases can be picked up in French flea markets and single crochet hooks are also fairly common. Elegant crochet hook sets, with perhaps cornelian handles, should be purchased. Plush velvet and leatherette cases with ordinary tools are not good investments as yet, as there are too many about.

A selection of plastic and bakelite sewing sets and hussifs. The two impressed bakelite cases showing scissors and thimbles are rare. $64-128/£40-80.

A selection of brass and aluminum advertising thimbles, which were given away with the product. They fetch around $13-19/£8-12 each, depending on condition and rarity.

Left: a plastic Coca-Cola advertising thimble. $10/£6. Right: a novelty thimble holder. $32/£20.

A selection of porcelain tools by Limoges: a needle case and a thimble case with matching thimble, hand-painted and gilded with ormolu mounts, c. 1980. Approximately $64/£40 each.

A silver and blue enamel single thimble and boxed set of three pieces, brought out by the Thimble Society as a memorial to the life and work of Diana, Princess of Wales.

American tools came into their own in the early twentieth century, two of the most prolific makers being Simons Bros. and Unger Bros. The United States does not have the same hallmarking system, just sterling silver and a trademark denoting the manufacturer. There is no date letter, so one has to estimate the date of manufacture. In thimbles, the trademark is nearly always found in the apex of the thimble. Typical tools to look out for would be hem measurers and thimble boxes with a hinged lid and central post. Just why there were so many hem measurers manufactured is puzzling. Of course, it is a much bigger country, but were women forever altering their hem lines? Glove darners and darners in general were also more popular in the States.

Of course, glove darners were used in Britain too, as women were not thought properly dressed without hat and gloves. However, collections of darners in all sorts of materials, such as glass and china, are more popular in the States. Winders in silver—especially in the shape of a cross—are typical, as are strawberry emeries with silver tops. Fish are one of the most frequently used attractive motifs, and can be found on shuttles, needle cases, and ribbon threaders. Ribbon threaders, which were used to pull ribbon through lingerie or summer dresses, are also more popular in the States, and can be most decorative, especially in boxed sets of varying sizes. Even the boxes were made in novelty shapes, such as hearts and shields. Beautiful thimbles were still being made during the early twentieth century in some quantity by Simons Bros., Ketcham & McDougal, Stern Bros. and many others.[2]

American shuttles often have hooks at the end, which were used to connect the rings of tatting together. An alternative method was to use a crochet hook, or even a hook suspended from a chain on a finger ring. The hook suspended from a ring is also found in many boxed tatting sets. Having one sharp end on your shuttle serves the same purpose. Bakelite tools, including shuttles, are becoming sought after in the States, especially the colored bakelite examples made in imitation mother-of-pearl. Most bakelite items are practically given away in England, so start collecting them now while they are still cheap. At the less costly end of the market, it's at least unlikely that one would enter into as risky a bargain as the one described on the next page, related to me by an American collector.

A typical early twentieth century plastic tatting shuttle from America showing a picture of the woman who was used to promote the products. It has an advertisement for patent medicines on the reverse. Note the one pointed end which was typical of American shuttles of that period. $128/£80.

This amusing story recounts the way that Tiffany got its elegant premises and is a good example of how vanity can lead us all astray! During the late nineteenth century, pearls reached the top of their value, never to be surpassed. This was mainly due to pearls being a favorite of royalty, especially Queen Mary. There was enormous rivalry amongst the wealthy American society hostesses of the time to have the biggest and best matching string. Tiffany had obtained a magnificent row of pearls, and two rival hostesses started to outbid each other for it. To clinch the deal, one woman said to Tiffany: "You can have my house in exchange for the necklace." At the time, their values would have been about equal. Now, however, the pearls would fetch only a little more than they did then, whereas the Tiffany premises are worth over five million pounds!

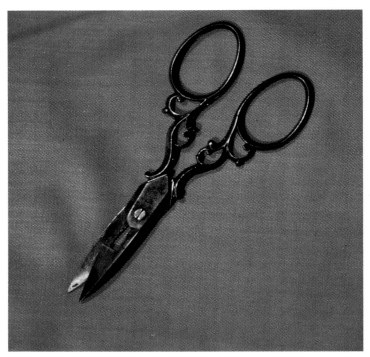

A pair of button-hole scissors in steel with elegant turn-of-the-century handles made by the famous Tiffany company in America, whose name is engraved above the screw. $128/£80.

Iron ore was mined near Philadelphia, where steel forges were set up, and steel scissors were made in the 1850s. Be on the lookout for steel scissors with cut out patterns showing birds, flowers, or even buildings. They are not finely done, like the French ones, but are vigorous and fun, and as yet not too pricey. Also in the north, you will find the Pennsylvania Dutch settlements, a generic name given to several different sects, such as the Shakers and the Amish. They live in a traditional manner, still having community barn-raising, and quilting bees. All their tools are simple, functional, and handmade. A typical sewing box or roll is made from two flat discs of wood covered in fabric, with padded fabric rolled around, attached, and sewn with cloth compartments for the tools. The roll can be unrolled to disclose the tools, then rolled up and tied with two ribbons. Because color and pattern is considered a sign of vanity, the rolls are always in monochrome brown or grey. Nevertheless, the old ones are fetching high prices, around $200-300 (£125-187). Quilts are the only exception to the color rule, as they are made from scraps.

American Samplers

American samplers are rare, and consequently expensive. They have a different history than those from Britain. In the States, samplers were made only by schoolgirls during school hours. American girls did not sit at home making samplers or doing embroidery. They were out clearing land and chopping wood. They learnt enough sewing to make clothes, and anything else needed for survival, but otherwise there were more vital concerns to attend to. The same applies to other pioneer settlements in Canada, New Zealand, Australia, and South Africa. A woman had to pull her weight in the fields, as well as in "huntin', shootin', and fishin'!" Many of the sewing tools that survive in old work boxes are homemade, in simple materials such as wood and bone. In themselves, they illustrate an interesting and different way of life, one which was tremendously hard, but at least involved working your own land.

As the twentieth century draws to a close, technology is spreading into all walks of life. One might think that hand sewing has become a thing of the past, but perhaps in order to balance all the mechanization, sewing groups are becoming increasingly popular. A friend of mine has just finished traveling, and remarked how many women she had met in America, Canada, New Zealand, Australia, and South Africa who regularly attended sewing get-togethers. Many of them quilted, embroidered pictures, and made clothing they had designed themselves. In rural areas, such get-togethers made for a companionable way to spend a creative evening. The tools they used were a mixture of old and new, but some of them had amazing collections of antique tools collected over many years.

Collecting antique sewing tools has only just begun to be appreciated and to take its place amongst the important antique items already established. I do hope that I have been able to pass on some of my enthusiasm in this book, and introduce new friends to a subject that will give them lasting pleasure and interest all their lives.

Chapter Seven

Private Collections

This part of the book is devoted to selected items of interest from several private collections. The owners of these collections have been kind enough to share their wonderful items for use in the book.

From the Behr Collection, Northern Ireland

The owner of this collection provided the following description of how she began collecting needlework tools and the pleasure she derives from her hobby:

How did I start collecting needlework tools? Some years ago, whilst searching in a local antique shop for vaseline glass, I found a little leather case with a folding brass holder inside. The proprietor explained that she had bought it from an old lady who said it had been for dance cards—a sort of *carnet de bal*. Certainly there were numbers on the different sections but they ranged from six to twelve, which seemed a little strange. I put it with my other little personal treasures and forgot about it.

About a year later I was in Birmingham on business and decided to treat myself to an extra day in order to visit an antique fair where a glass dealer friend of mine had a stand. I wandered round the fair and there, on a stand full of pin cushions, scissors, tape measures, and strange but beautiful bits of mother-of-pearl, was a little brass case just like mine. I asked the stallholder why, if it was for dance cards, the numbers started at six and she informed me that it was the first brass needle case to be patented and that it was called a "Beatrice."

That lady has a lot to answer for! Business wasn't exactly brisk and she spent the next hour telling me about all the wonderful things she had on her stand. I was mesmerized, and since then have been obsessed with Georgian and Victorian needlecases, mother-of-pearl thread winders, Lady's Companions, cut steel scissors, Palais Royale workboxes, ivory needle books, and the hundred and one things connected with needlework.

Some are practical, everyday working implements and some are so delicate that they were obviously never intended to be used. Who made them? Who were they made for? Who used them? What stories could they tell? These questions led me to become interested in the so-

cial history. It is such a joy to discover an old sewing box complete with the entire contents—it tells you so much about the life of the person or the family who owned it. Unfortunately, the contents are more often missing. I recently found a beautiful, but empty, box in a shop which sells antique furniture. The dealer explained that it had come from a house clearance, but there had been nothing interesting inside so he'd dumped the contents in a rubbish bin. He then proceeded to describe scraps of lace and beadwork, old buttons, and bits of ivory, which, if his descriptions were correct, were a tambour hook and two lucets.

Where do I find new material? Many of my friends also collect small antiques, so we run a sort of co-operative. I look out for vesta cases, inkwells, fans, and other items for them and they look out for needlework implements for me. One in particular travels a lot and often brings me back exciting things. Several of the local antique dealers know what I collect and (so long as they recognize the items) keep them for me.

What will happen to my collection when I die? My son and son-in-law both refer to it as junk! My daughter appreciates what I have but would probably still sell it. I need to educate my two little granddaughters to look after it and, if possible, to add to it. I've started a collection of miniature shoes for one granddaughter and one of little trade scent bottles for the other. They are fairly easy to find, inexpensive, and not too easily broken. Once my granddaughters have developed the habit, I hope they will get as much pleasure from it as I have. Building a collection (of anything) is such a fascinating and worthwhile hobby that I can't imagine life without it.

An old peddler bear called Mini is the inspiration behind this collection. Nobody knows Mini's age but she is probably around ninety years old. A battered bird's feather is stuck in her headband, and she is hung about with bits of lace, ribbons, buttons, needles, and pins. The original label is still attached to her pedestal.

A small copper measure for the thirsty needlewoman, along with a selection of nineteenth and early twentieth century tools, some Irish and some imported. Note the linen buttons, an industry by which a poor woman could augment her income.

Leather cases: scissors, thimble case, and a shagreen covered étui.

All these articles are miniatures, the mother-of-pearl sewing box at the back measuring 4".

Further miniatures in metal, most items measuring under 1".

A large, painted wooden Irish sewing box, c. 1830, the contents of which are all original. The box has remained a family possession, hence the packed interior in the bottom half. This is the best condition in which to find a box, with so much history to be gleaned from reading through all the items.

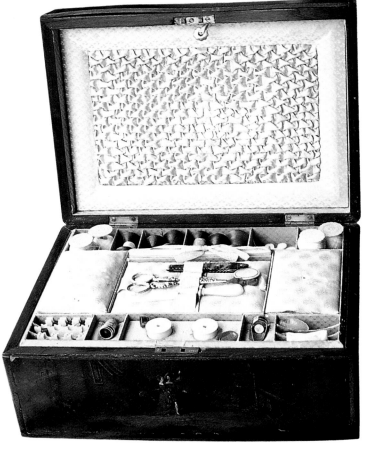

Inside of the box.

Opposite page, top and bottom: Here are some of the articles found inside the Irish sewing box.

More articles found inside the box from page 158.

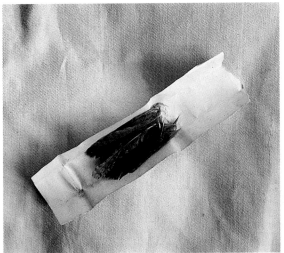

Tiny bird feathers found inside the sewing box from page 158, with a note sent from on board ship, describing the bird.

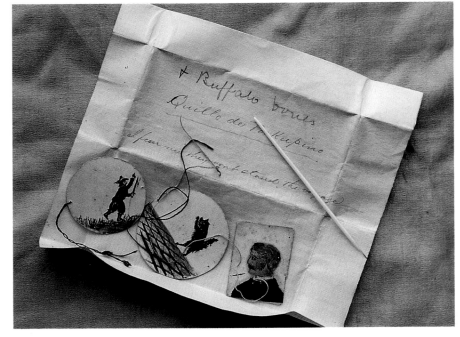

Letter home from the sender of the feathers and quills, with information regarding the flora and fauna of a sea voyage.

Brass Avery needle cases, c. 1880.

Irish traveling sewing machine.

Various ivory needle cases, needle books, and silver châtelaine clip.

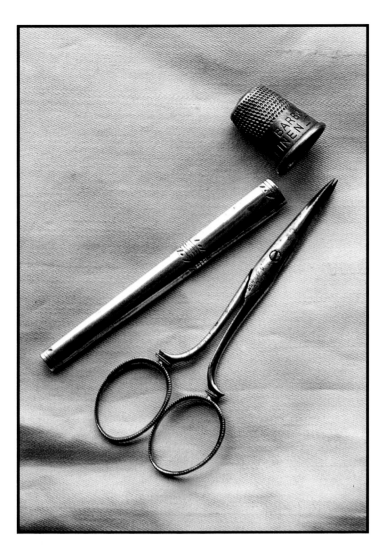

Irish silver needle case, steel scissors, and advertising thimble from a local store.

Steel clamp, c. 1830.

Rare cherub clamp.

A selection of Averys, needle cases, and Mauchlin.

Miniature pin holder, size 1.5".

Miniature needle cases and pin cushions on the corner of a lace handkerchief, all items 1.5".

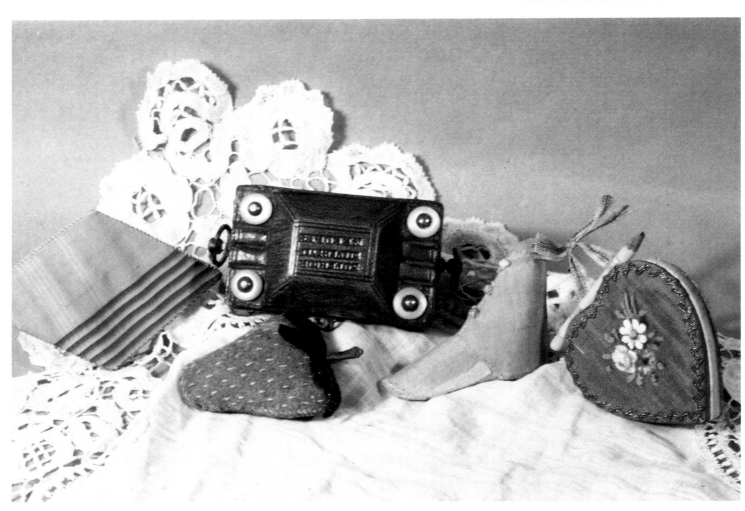

Two doll's hats, and miniature needle boxes, c. 1825.

Silver pin cushion in the
shape of a chair.

Redditch needle case counter display holder.

A variety of tools.

A selection of winders.

Twentieth century tools: a donkey and a
Dutch girl, bakelite tapes, a cardboard
unfolding sewing set.

The owner of this collection wishes to remain anonymous. The collection has been formed over nearly twenty years and is elegantly displayed in an early nineteenth century drawing room overlooking a charming garden in Southern Ireland.

Papier mâché inlaid with mother-of-pearl, after the style of Jennens and Bethridge, c. 1860.

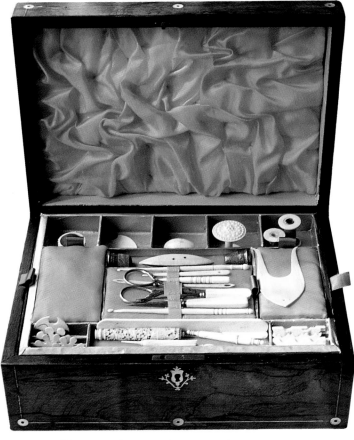

Rosewood box, ivory fittings with a lucet and Cantonese needle case, c. 1850.

Ebony inlaid with ivory, possibly made in India for the British Raj, fitted with ivory tools.

The box above open.

Rosewood box, with mother-of-pearl tools.

Various tools and needle packets.

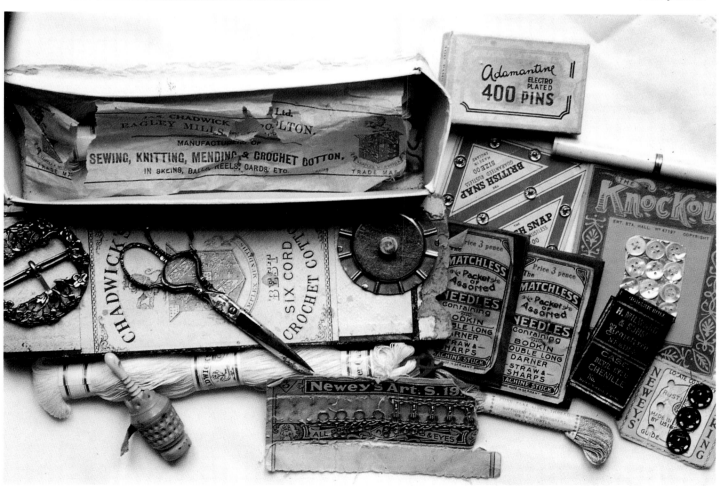

Ivory tools on Irish white work.

Châtelaines and tools.

A cloth châtelaine and a brass pattern stencil.

Mother-of-pearl Palais Royal tools. Note the unusual flowers enameled on the scissors handles.

A lovely mother-of-pearl fitted
box, with the crest of a
Viscountess on the lid.

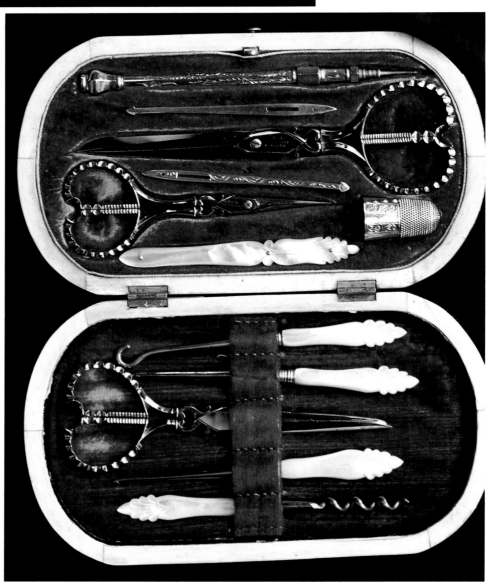

The inside of the box with fitted
mother-of-pearl and steel tools.

Coramandel wooden box fitted with mother-of-pearl, c. 1860.

Ebony and mother-of-pearl box.

Inside fitted with mother-of-pearl tools.

Leather box with gold tooling.

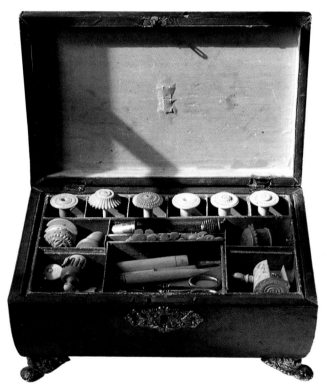

Mixed fittings inside.

Mother-of-pearl fittings, c. 1860.

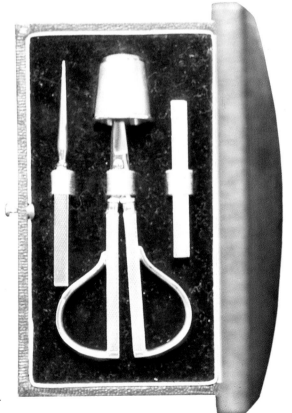

Art Deco silver sewing set.

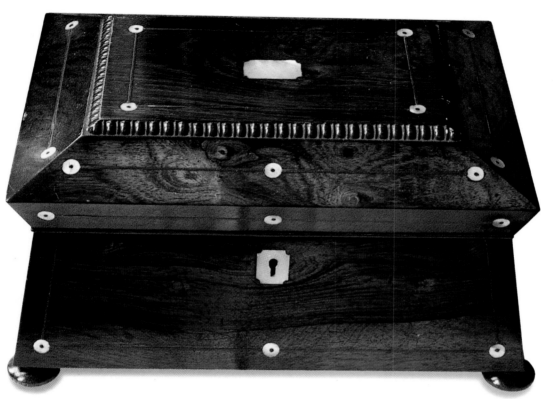

Rosewood and mother-of-pearl box.

Vegetable ivory tools inside
the box.

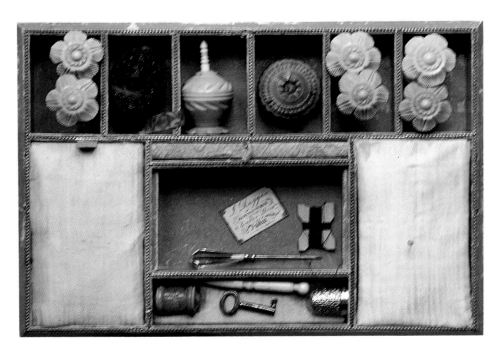

Opposite page:
Top: Sewing sets and a
boxed netting set with
winder.

Bottom: Two plate
châtelaines and two Nanny
pin brooches.

Close-up of tools from page 175.

Old silk trimmings.

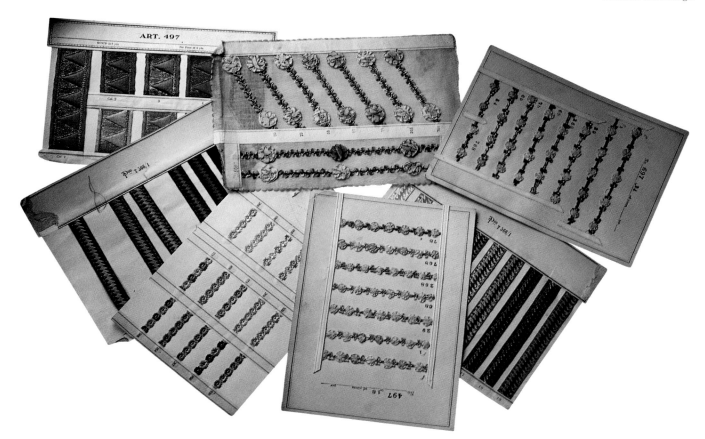

Wooden clamps, a knitting sheath, and a knitting needle holder at the bottom.

Various vegetable ivory tools.

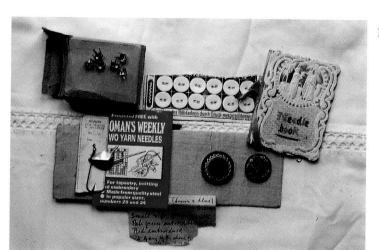

Linen buttons and needle packets.

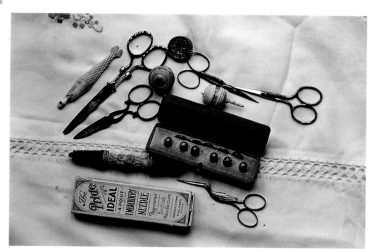

Scissors and tools.

Old silks, a silver ivory-mounted glove stretcher, and a
bookmark in Bristol board ready to be embroidered.

Mr. Hedley Smith has been collecting for approximately ten years. During that time, he has bought around eight fitted sewing boxes, as well as countless tools. Working full time in London, he takes whatever free time he has to go to auctions and to search for items in the nearest antique markets. The main focus of his collection is on boxes, with the accent on the items inside, particularly ephemera. Hedley Smith tries to find boxes that have old bits of silk, old letters, paper needle cases: in short the perishable bits of history that usually get thrown away or lost over the years.

Georgian mahogany sewing box with contents. The contents are illustrated in the photo below.

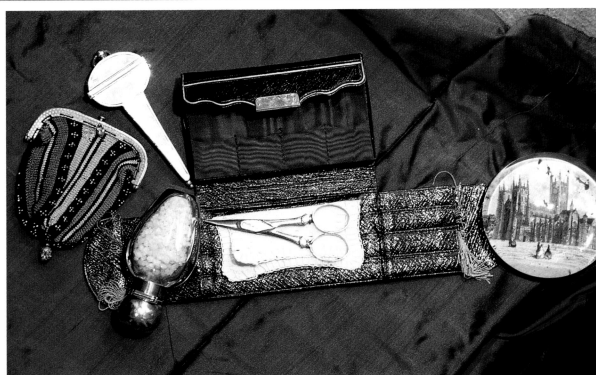

A military Moroccan leather unfolding sewing kit, and other items.

Doll, and leaves from a monthly almanac.

Another doll, various pieces of embroidery, and some dolls' clothes.

Regency leather sewing box, with silk transfer print decorations.

A multiplication table, tiny miniature boots half an inch long, bead bags, a cut paper needle book, and old letters, c. 1830.

Extremely fine paper cut picture, often found in sewing boxes and possibly used as a stencil.

Mementos from a needle box, c. 1812. Most articles less than 1.5" across.

Miniature items, most just under an inch. See the finger
guard and corner of the lace handkerchief for scale.

Fashion cards for ladies' hats. Each
hat design slides over the picture of
the face to show how it will look
when worn—a very sensible idea.

A publication called *The World of Fashion*.

Miniature doll in a box, and a
needle case with an imitation
watch as decoration.

Various tiny needle packets and
cases, each not more than an inch.

A silver kettle tape, a châtelaine, an étui, and
a boxed sewing set, c.1850.

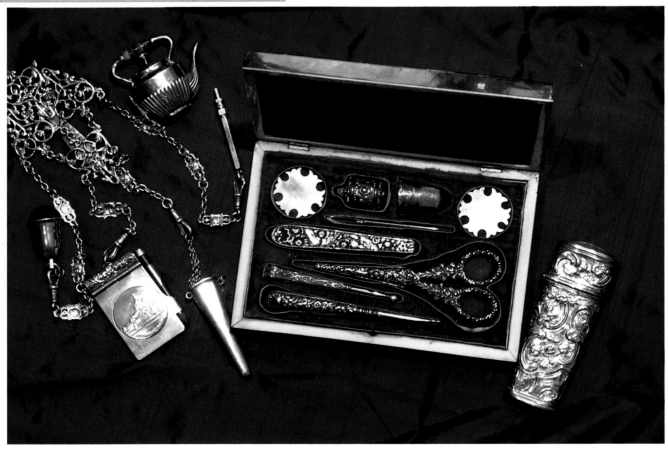

Here is a collection of sewing items, ranging in price from $1.00 (50p) up to $112 (£70). Pam has a very keen eye, but a limited budget, rarely spending over $25 (£40) for a tool, and more often a few pence! Car boot sales, church halls, charity shops, thrift shops, local garden jumble sales, general antique fairs—nowhere is excluded as the possible source of a bargain! Consequently her collection is full of the unexpected. Well-used working tools sit alongside homemade items; there is so much of individual interest.

A brass, shoe-shaped needle case, probably an Avery, and three more pin wheels.

Five flat pin wheels, three early nineteenth century and two later advertising pin wheels.

Four Mauchlin pin cushions, c. 1870, and a central ivory one.

Pam's specialty is making tiny teddy-bears, here seated
with a thimble and a stiletto.

A leather needle and pin case, c. 1900.

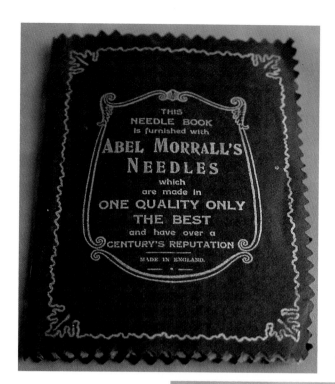

Abel Morall's needle case.

Same case, opened.

A printed glass pin holder, a
paper cut-out decorated needle
case, and another needle book.

Four delightful needle books, late nineteenth and early twentieth century.

A selection of needle cases. Left to right: bakelite, Cantonese carved ivory, wood, a metal hussif, black lacquer, silver, paper, carved ivory. In the lower center, early nineteenth century leather.

Outer row, from left: a Tunbridge waxer, a vegetable ivory tape, a mother-of-pearl spool holder, a vegetable ivory tape, an ivory cotton barrel. Center: a butterfly spring loaded tape, a flower decorated spring loaded tape. Bottom row: a vegetable ivory wax holder, a Cantonese ivory carved clamp, a mother-of-pearl wax holder.

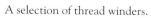

A selection of thread winders.

An embroidered needle box.

A silk printed view of Lambeth Bridge,
London, on a pin cushion, c. 1850.

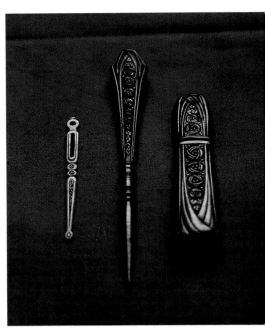

A bodkin, stiletto,
and needle case,
French, c. 1890-1900.

Beaded velvet pin cushion c. 1860.
2"/5cm.

Nineteenth century pin cushions.

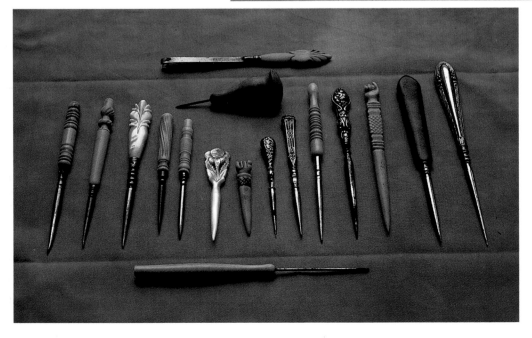

A selection of nineteenth
century prickers and stilettos.

From the Helen Eastgate Collection, Wales and London, U.K.

Over the last twenty years, Helen Eastgate has amassed a fascinating collection of tools and thimbles. The range of her collection is eclectic, both in extent and in variety of subject and object. Helen has traveled all over the world, especially in the Near, Middle, and Far East, bringing back such items as châtelaines and needle cases from China and rare thimbles from Turkestan.

Novelty thimble cases, late nineteenth century.

Tunbridge ware cotton holders, along with combined waxer, pin cushion, and tape, c. 1840.

Silver pin cushions inspired by tennis.

Novelty pin cushion.

Rare metal tape-measure, late
nineteenth century.

Two novelty needle cases.

A Dorcas-inspired cotton reel holder.

Front view of the Dorcas reel holder.

Needle cases.

Lid of a Tunbridge sewing box, c. 1840. See tools inside on opposite page.

Victorian silver badges and brooches. These are very often found in sewing boxes, collected and given to family members.

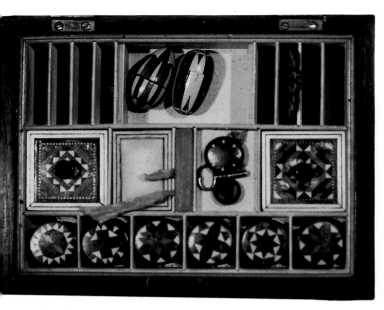

Inside of the sewing box from page 196, fitted with Tunbridge tools.

Various Victorian commemorative
pin cushions.

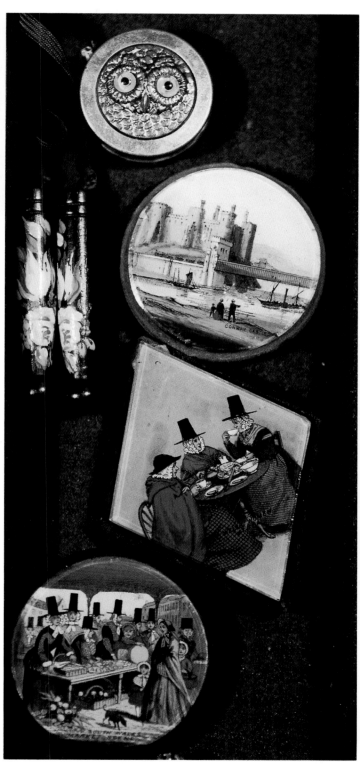

Glass pin cushions, with colored engravings—
the pins go around the side, c. 1860.

More needle cases: Edward and
Alexandra plus two others of
Queen Victoria.

Victorian needle cases, featuring Queen Victoria and Prince Albert.

Various pin cushions, tapes,
and thimble holders.

An unusual needle case inside an embroidered sleeve.

Chinese silver novelty needle cases, the tops attached with cords.

More Chinese needle cases.

Two needle cases from China, the man in lacquer opening at the waist.

Two Chinese thimble rings or finger guards, along with needle and pin holders.

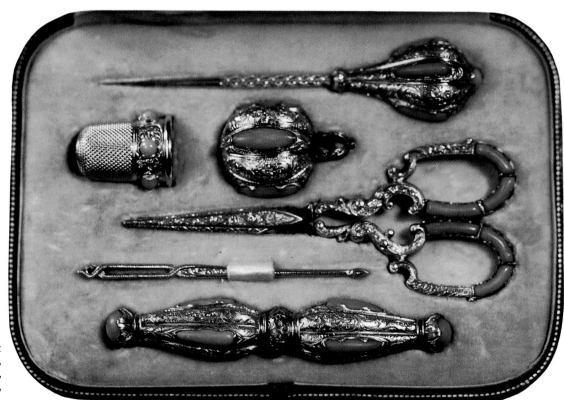

Coral and silver-gilt sewing set, c. 1840, containing a stiletto, thimble, tape, scissors, bodkin, and needle case.

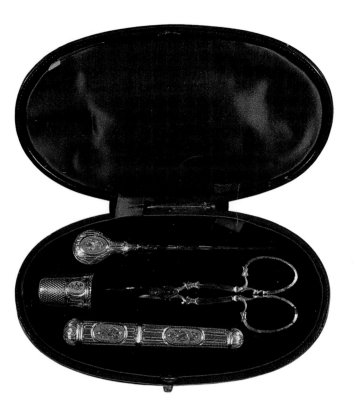

French Empire, gold and
enamel boxed set.

Gold and mother-of-pearl boxed set with two snow
flake winders, a penknife, needle case, scissors,
thimble, bodkin, hook and stiletto, and scent bottle.

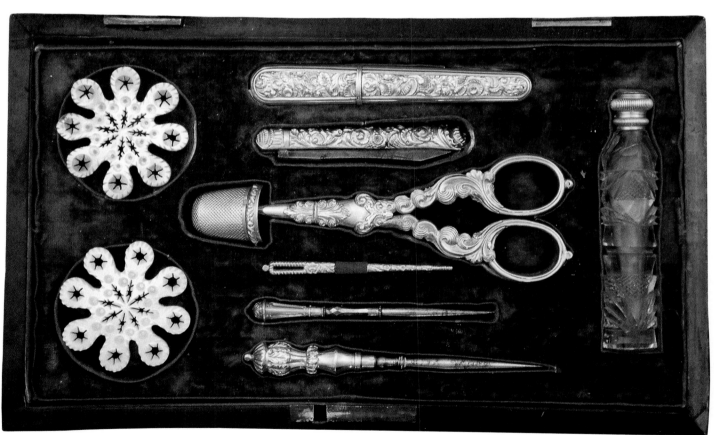

Group of eighteenth century enamel tools: two needle cases, an egg thimble case, and two thimbles.

Enamel on gold bodkin case, possibly a letter wax holder, probably French, late eighteenth century. Sealing wax was kept in long holders, the wax being taken out and melted under a candle flame, dropped onto an envelope, and impressed with one's seal.

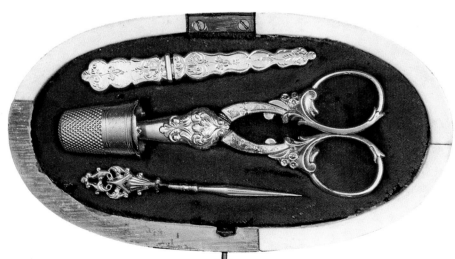

A gold sewing set, c. 1840.

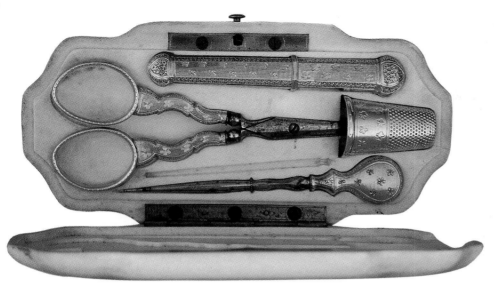

A silver-gilt French set,
c.1850, in a fitted ivory box.

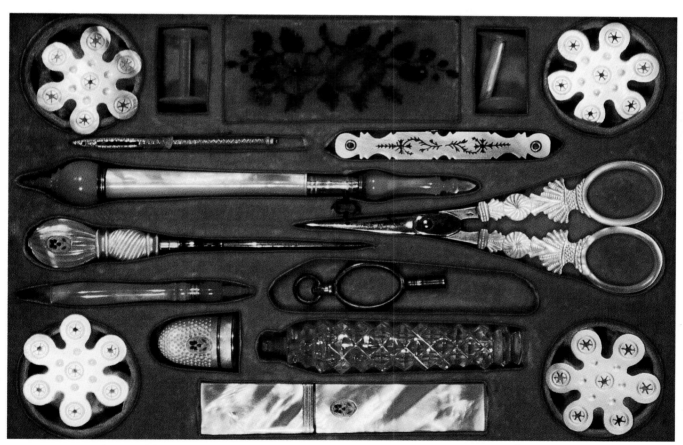

A Palais Royal fitted box, with four flat winders, two cylindrical winders, bodkin, ear-spoon and tooth pick,
tambour hook, scissors, stiletto, a pricker possibly for lace work, a thimble, scent bottle, and needle case.

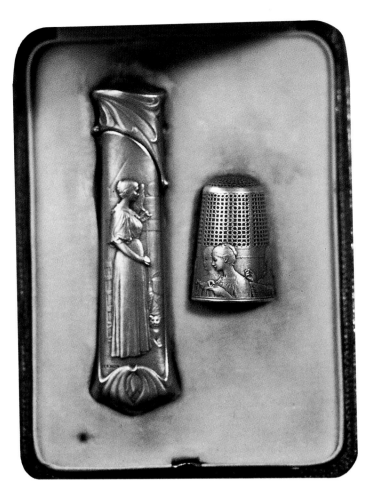

A French Art Nouveau silver boxed set, in the manner of the Sewing Girls, a very famous thimble design by Vernon of Paris. The original design was done at the turn of the nineteenth century and illustrated in *Les Modes* 1909.

Needle cases, tortoise tape, and thimble holder.

Enamel and porcelain thimble holders.

Norwegian David Andersen enamel étui with swan, a silver articulated fish compendium, a rare silver thimble toy with scent bottle, and a very rare eighteenth century needle case and gold thimble.

Molly Pearce is a knowledgable collector and researcher, especially concerning sewing items made in Sheffield plate. Working in an executive position for the City Museum, and with their kind co-operation, Molly has provided these interesting photos along with a history of the tools shown. It is very rare to find Sheffield plate items, therefore they are highly valued.

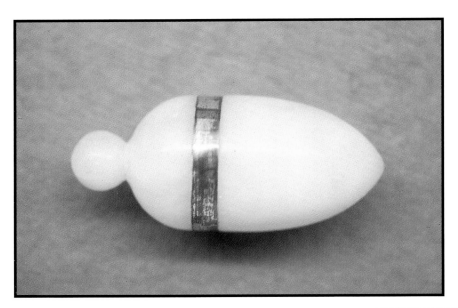

Derbyshire alabaster thimble holder with central band of Old Sheffield plate, 2" long. Chellaston near Derby was famous for its alabaster quarries, used in the Middle Ages for figure carving by artists from Nottingham and Burton-on-Trent. One of the best examples is the monument to Godfrey Poljambe and his wife in Bakewell Church (1385).

Old Sheffield plate knitting sheath love token with silver surface on the front only, copper edge disguised by silver wire, 2.75" long. The bright cut engraving, suggesting a date of c. 1800, involved cutting quite deeply into the silver surface and required plated sheet with an extra thick surface. According to Peter Brears, who wrote the standard article on knitting sheaths, heart-shaped sheaths of this type were popular in the Aire valley between Keighley and Bradford in Yorkshire. The sheath was intended to be sewn onto a pad of cloth, which could then be sewn or pinned onto the clothing or held in place by a tape tied around the body.

Old Sheffield plate waistcoat buttons, c. 1780, diameter .75". Eighteenth century metal buttons often have a bone center with a criss-cross piece of gut for sewing them onto the clothing. The decoration on the metal front was stamped on with the help of a steel die; the edge was then turned over to secure the bone center while the button was revolving on a lathe.

Old Sheffield plate étui, length 3.5", silver on one surface only, c. 1780. Hand-chased rococo decoration done while the metal was still flat, then bent into shape. Reeded silver wire at closure. No contents.

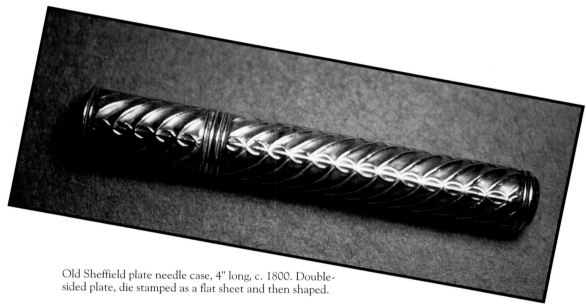

Old Sheffield plate needle case, 4" long, c. 1800. Double-sided plate, die stamped as a flat sheet and then shaped.

Old Sheffield plate spool knave, 6" long, c. 1780. Unusual plated wire work, sometimes used to make cake baskets or wine coasters. Thin sheet of silver was fused onto a round bar of copper which was then drawn as thin as needed.

Most of the tools shown here are no longer in Betty's possession, but she has had the pleasure of finding and researching the items before releasing them through her business over the last ten years. Betty has nearly always gone for the rich and the rare, concentrating on top quality pieces, often of continental origin. In 1997, Betty formed a firm of antique dealers under the name of Betty Aardewerk & Sons, working mainly in Holland though exhibiting in fairs both in England and America.

A very rare needle case in pewter excavated in the northern Netherlands and made in 1642, as evidenced by the mark at the top, 2.5" long. The reverse bears the initials "I.O.D." in a shield. The needle case is decorated with flowers and vines influenced by Spanish design, since at that time—the first quarter of the seventeenth century—the Spanish invaders had just been routed from the Low Countries. Note the twisted rope border motif, which is also found on seventeenth century thimbles. Note also the handles on either side through which cord was threaded so that the top did not get lost from the lower half. These cases were worn suspended from the waist. Many sewing tools worn in this way should be seen as dress accessories as well as sewing tools.

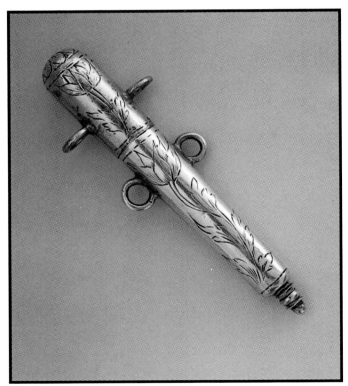

A silver needle case made in the second half of the seventeenth century. Note the tulip design and the same side handles for a cord as on the previous needle case. In Holland, during the height of fashion when tulips first became popular, a tulip bulb could cost the same amount as a house.

A needle case in ivory, probably Dieppe
work, showing a cornucopia. Note the crisp
detail, depth of carving, and realistic
portrayal of the fruit.

Ivory needle case, probably from Dieppe, 4"
long. It depicts Josephine Beauharnais, the
first wife of Napoleon Bonaparte, wearing
her coronation robes. The coronation of
Napoleon and his Empress Josephine took
place in 1804, and the robes were designed
by the court painter, Davide. The production was staged by the most famous actor of
the day, Tadema.

Late eighteenth century mother-of-pearl French needle case, probably from Paris, 4" long. It shows a sphinx and a delightful cupid's head at the base. The cornucopia opens halfway down to take the needles.

This *frivolité* is a little Palais Royal boxed set. The original label is still inside, reading "Grandeber Au Petit, Dunkerque, Richelieu No. 91, A Paris." It is in the shape of a flower basket and the top of the lid is engraved with a further flower basket. The tools inside are a scent bottle, scissors, thimble, and needle case. Betty Aardewerk notes that in France, gentlemen could purchase a "frivolity" in the shape of a butterfly embroidered with gold thread. This was given to ladies in order to stop them from unpicking gentlemen's epaulettes when they took out their drizzling sets. The butterfly contained the same length of gold thread, and was a more gallant way of stopping the pillage.

A miniature spool knave measuring only 1.5". In Dutch, the name for miniature objects was *poppegoet*. These objects were made for cabinets, which themselves were shaped like large doll's houses with glass fronts through which you could see all the little toys for grown-ups. The most famous painters and silversmiths of the day made these tiny objects as exact replicas of items found in rich merchants' houses. The merchants lived alongside the canals in Amsterdam, where their wives would try to outdo each other with their toy cabinet displays. Some of these houses are open to view today. Eighteenth century silversmiths, such as Johannes van Geffen, 1767-1788, Amsterdam (a member of the great van Geffen family), were famous for making these miniatures.

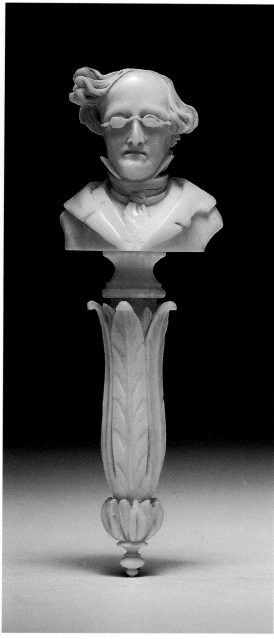

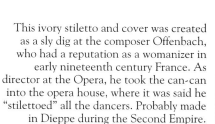

This ivory stiletto and cover was created as a sly dig at the composer Offenbach, who had a reputation as a womanizer in early nineteenth century France. As director at the Opera, he took the can-can into the opera house, where it was said he "stilettoed" all the dancers. Probably made in Dieppe during the Second Empire.

Opposite page: A sewing clamp in brass, steel, and gilded
steel with a bird made out of real feathers in the center.
The cage and the bird were symbols of a woman's virtue.
If a woman was keen on her suitor then she would bring
the bird out of the cage. If she did not want to receive his
advances she put the bird back in.

Palais Royal box with a musical movement in the base that plays two melodies from the opera *William Tell*. There is an ormolu plaque cast with a scene from the opera, showing William Tell, his son, and the famous apple. These souvenir boxes were made in the first year of the opera's production.

A clamp in steel decorated with gold. This decorative technique was called Tula work in eighteenth century Russia. When a new invention or style came out in Russia, it was the custom to present it for approval to the Tsar and Tsarina. If they bought pieces as presents the style would then become fashionable. Catherine the Great loved Tula work and so it became immensely popular.

Two views of a pierced bone clamp. This decorative technique was called Archangel work and originated in Russia on the coast north of Moscow. The port of Archangel was the Dieppe of Russia, famous for its carving in ivory and bone.

A silver-gilt, early eighteenth century compendium with a polychrome enamel figure of a tailor on the top. The matching thimble is at the side. After use, the thimble would be screwed back over the figure. The compendium unscrews in the usual manner, revealing a needle case and seal.

Filigree châtelaine, Dutch, early eighteenth century.
Note the much longer chains fashionable in
Holland, and the longer blades on the scissors.

An ivory corn-on-the-cob
mounted on silver as a
knitting-needle sheath.
Dutch, eighteenth century.

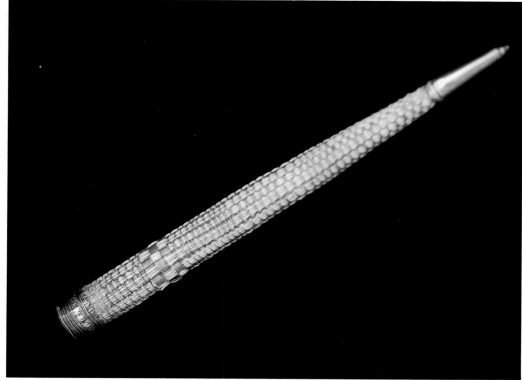

A steel, gun-metal gold and carnelian châtelaine. The item on the left is a fold or pleat maker. Continental, early nineteenth century.

All photos are courtesy of B.W.G. Wttewall, Holland, author of *Nederlands Klein Zilver*, published in 1987 by UITGEVERIJ ALLERT de LANGE, Amsterdam.

Silver filigree châtelaine with five pendants: a thimble holder c. 1790 by Adam; a bodkin and tweezers combined, c. 1760; scissors, c. 1752 by Adam; a needle case, and scent box, c. 1720 by Adam. The clip is also by Adam, 1740.

A scissors case, c. 1800.

Three scissors. From left: c. 1835, c. 1790, c. 1770.

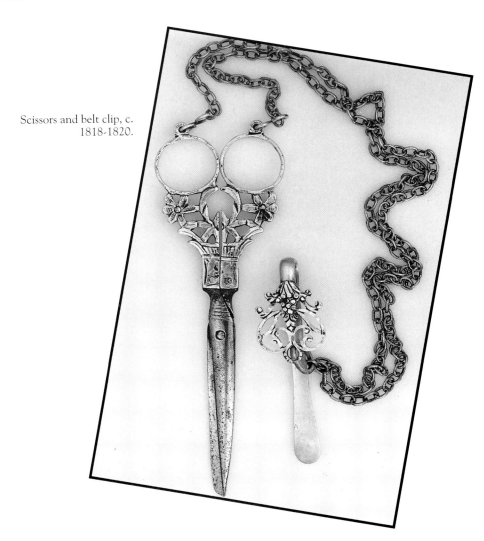

Scissors and belt clip, c. 1818-1820.

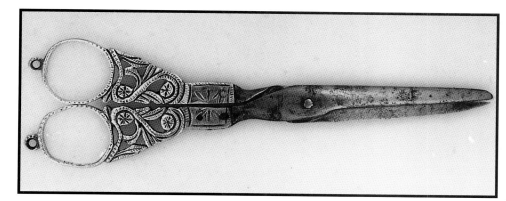

Scissors, c. 1830. Note the long blades.

Scissors case by Schavenkoker, c. 1680.

Knitting needle holder, c. 1782, by Dirk Hoep, Hoorn.

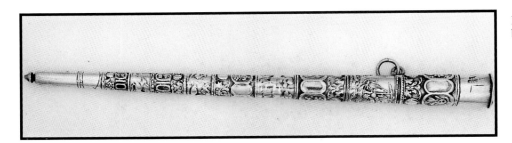

Knitting needle holder, c. 1736, by Adam.

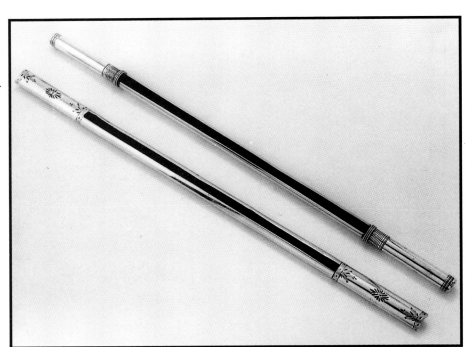

Knitting needle cases, c. 1807-1809.

Thimble and pin holder, c. 1840.

Hanging compendium for cotton and needles, c. 1740.

A pin-ball for holding pins, c. 1811-1812. In Holland, silver pin-balls on chains remained in use longer than in England.

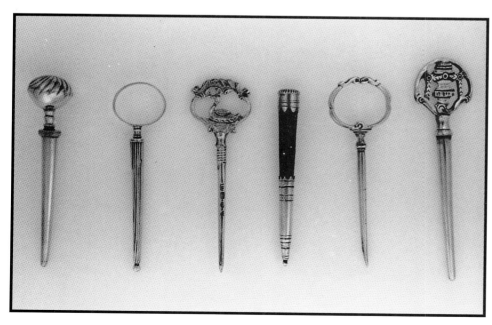

A group of stilettos and their covers, c. 1820.

A Dutch silver thimble
with cherubs, c. 1700.

A fine spool knave, c. 1792, to suspend
from a waist-clip and hold your thread.

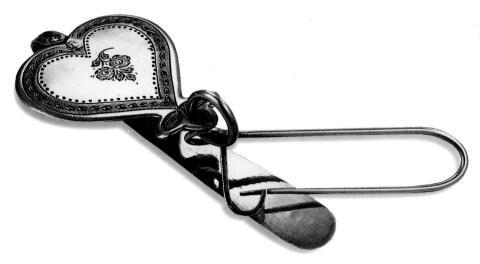

A waist clip and prong to hold wool or thread, c. 1868.

A bodkin box and bodkins, c. 1750, and a pin box.

A filigree bracelet and wool/thread holder, c. 1790-1820.

Ruth Mann has been collecting for the last twenty-five years. Working and living in the United States, Ruth concentrated on tools, especially châtelaines, clamps, and interesting items with a history, such as knitting sheaths. Traveling extensively in Europe as well as in America has enabled Ruth to buy many rare, good quality tools; she always looks for those in top condition.

Plain box with porcelain portrait, metal frame and edges.

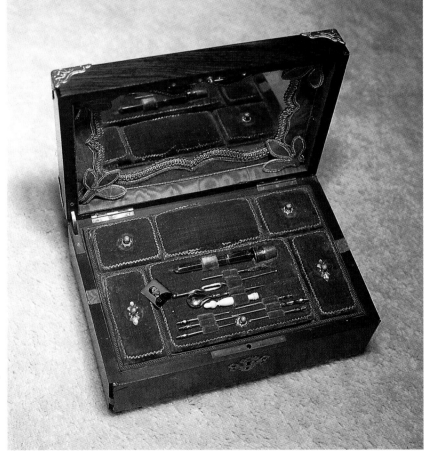

The inside of the box is blue velvet with gold trim, and includes a small picture of the lady who owned it—a member of the Glidden family of Marblehead, Massachusetts (owners of Glidden Paint Co).

Three miniature tool boxes. The one on the left has a
raised, stuffed, and embroidered emery on top, the one
in the middle is a Ladies Companion. In the front, a
French leather and gold tooled roll.

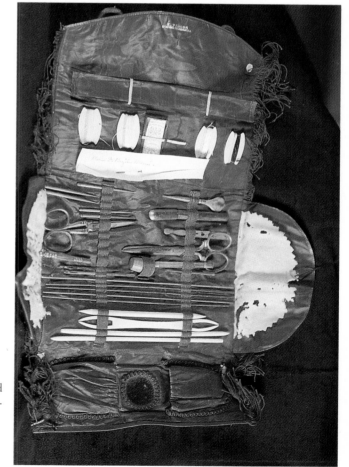

The roll opened, showing brass and
ivorine crochet and netting tools.

A very unusual Indian box
with three colored ivory insets.

Selection of opened sewing sets.

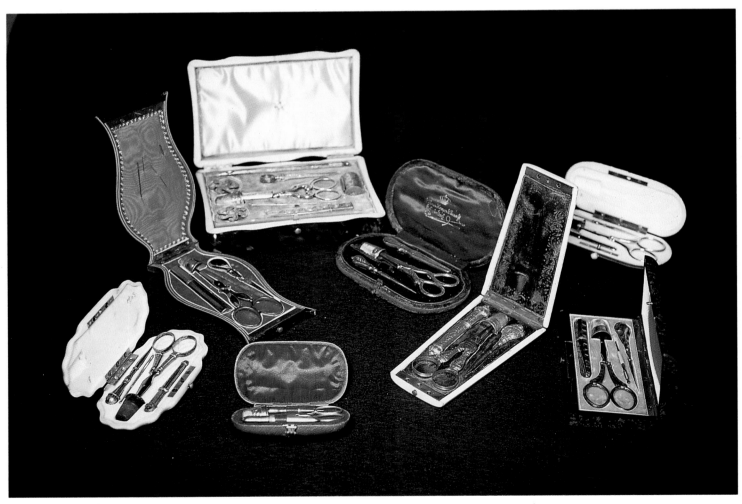

Another Ladies
Companion.

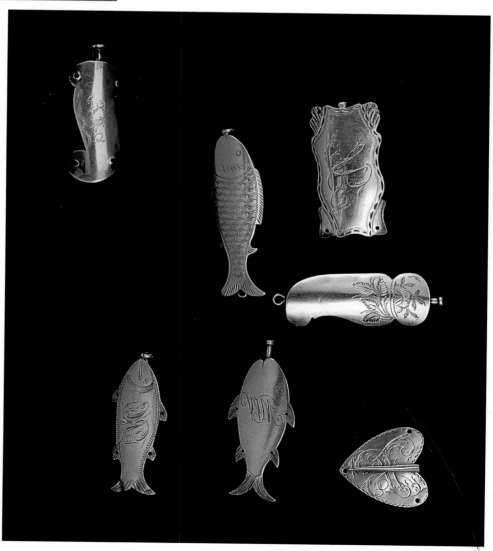

A group of silver knitting
sheaths. Note the holes around
the outside where they were
sewn onto aprons.

Vegetable ivory box with vegetable ivory thread winders.

An American sterling silver winder in a cross form, typical of America, c. 1890.

American silver winders, c. 1890.

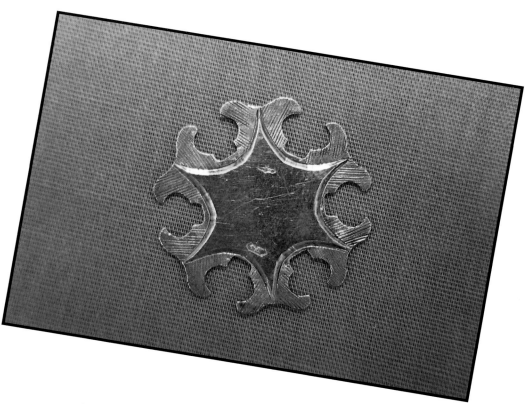

American silver winders, c. 1890.

American silver winders, c. 1890.

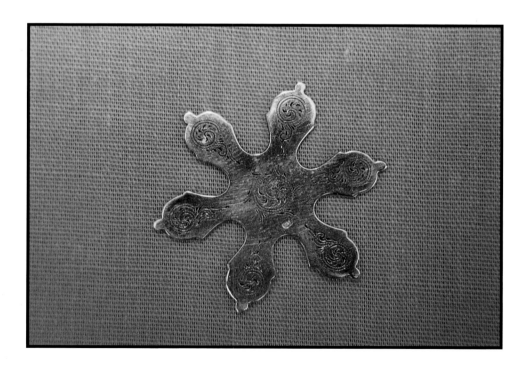

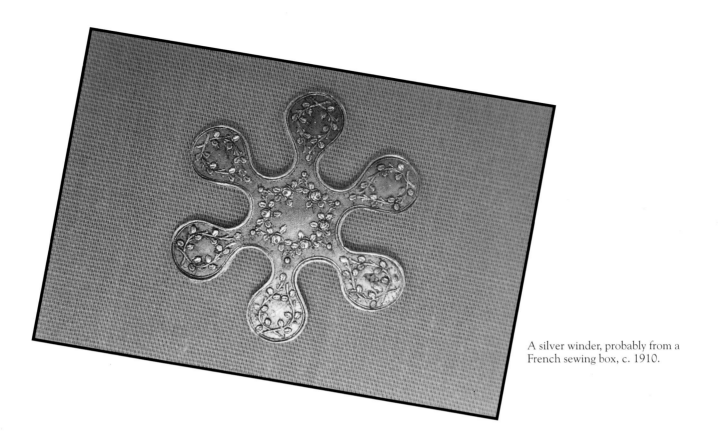

A silver winder, probably from a
French sewing box, c. 1910.

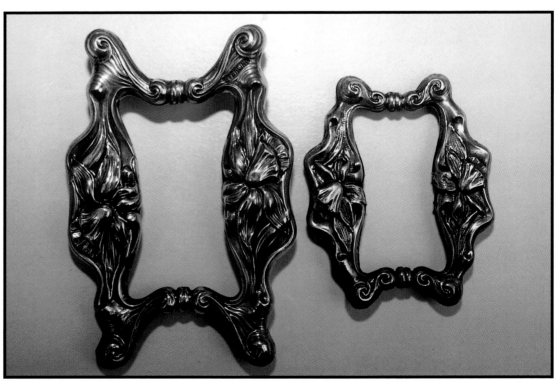

Two American silver winders with a strong Art Nouveau design.

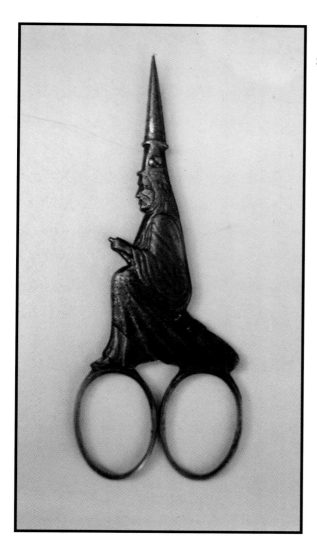

Salem witch scissors in metal.

A rare Amish needle holder, 2"
long, in silver, c. 1900.

A turtle-shaped, brass
advertising tape-measure.

A stiletto in the shape of a fish, made by Simons in silver, 2" long, c. 1890-1900.

Wendy Ritchie has provided photos of whatever Australian tools she could find, which admittedly were not many, but were gladly included. Wendy also mentioned a booklet for collectors called *Early Australian Samplers 1831-1940*, published by The Embroiderers Guild, Victoria, Australia. Wendy herself has a fine collection, including many British and European items.

A wool winder with heavy base made of Huon pine—a much prized wood native to Tasmania. The second photo is an close-up of the finial, on the top of which is a small bead of wood engraved with leaves and "CHRISTMAS 1904." Diameter of the wooden base is 5".

A wooden needle case decorated with the painting of a Blue Wren (one of Australia's tiny native birds) with "NEEDLES" painted down the other side, 3.5" long. The thimble is plastic. Many of these were made in the 1940s and 1950s.

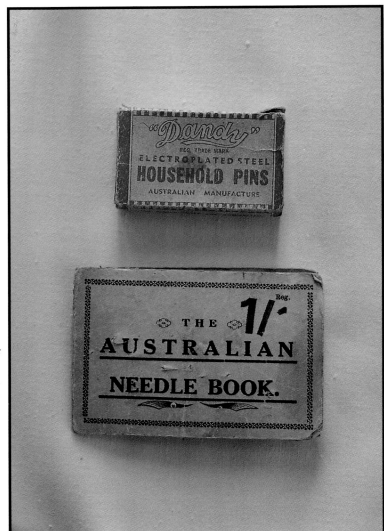

Top: a cardboard box of "Dandy" Household pins of Australian manufacture, 2.75" x 1.75". Bottom: "The Australian Needle Book"—cardboard with flannel leaves, containing a packet of Abel Morrall's celebrated needles. 10.25" x 7".

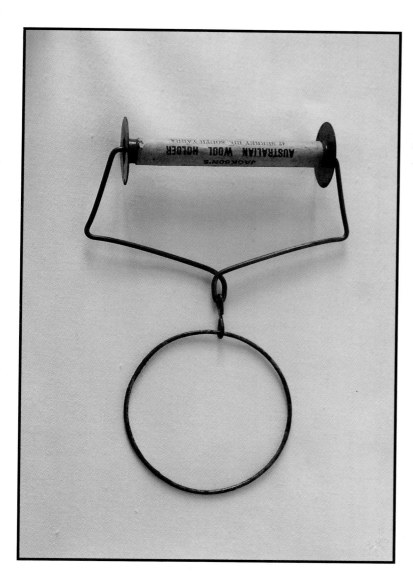

"The Australia Wool Holder" with ring and reel of blue painted steel, the remaining metal unfinished. Pink cardboard around the reel reads "No. 6822 Protected Patent applied for. Jackson's Australian Wool Holder. 47 Surrey Road, South Yarra." 5" at widest point, diameter of ring 3".

9 ct. gold thimble, ribbon threader, and fine crochet hook and sheath made in Melbourne by Palfrey in the 1930s. His mark was F9.

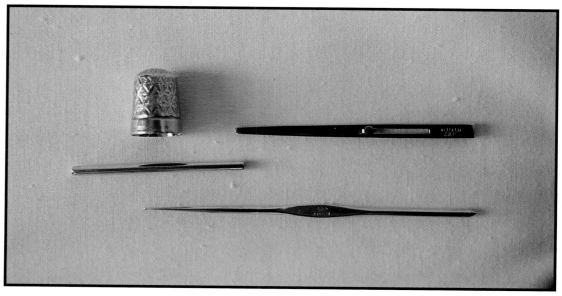

Three matching wooden winders handmade by J. Henley Snr., 29-4-1902, with Michmond House, Milawa on the front and Milawa P.O. on the reverse. 3" x 2".

A small embroidered needle book depicting English garden flowers, Australian-made in the 1930s.

Needle book with glass picture depicting "Sandridge Williams Town," a beach suburb of Melbourne, now called Williamstown. Inside the back cover it has pockets for 6, 7, 8, and 9 needles; inside the front (glass) cover is a flannel leaf for needles. 3.5" x 2".

China pin tray with "TASMANIA" and a red lion crest. Made by Arcadian, Stoke on Trent for the Australian market. 3.75" x 2.75"

Appendix I

Textile Craft Techniques

In order to understand how some sewing tools were used, here is a short explanation of various textile craft techniques.

Knotting

Knotting is similar to macramé and tatting. Like macramé, a series of knots is made in the length of the thread using a large shuttle, passing back and forth. The shuttle has to be large owing to the thick thread often used. The resulting length of knots could be used for several purposes, the most typical being for fringes, either looped or in some cases cut. The knots can be so fine and close to each other that the effect looks like a rich raised embroidery. Knotting has been done since the sixteenth century. Dr. Caius himself is said to have given a knotted cushion to Gonville and Caius College, Cambridge, in 1558. By the eighteenth century, knotting was a pastime undertaken by aristocratic ladies who wanted to give the appearance of working. The finest collection of knotting shuttles is to be found in The Wallace Collection in London.

Netting

Nets in all their various forms have been made since there were things to be caught. Snaring fish or birds, or ensnaring men with fine net covering a décolletage, were some of their uses, as were covering a simple silk dress or tying a net around one's bonnet allowing lashes to be fluttered alluringly through it. Netting formed the base for sixteenth and seventeenth century filet lace. In the nineteenth century, innumerable purses, mats, hair decorations, and other knickknacks were netted. Knotted fringing was used to trim netted bed hangings. Hand netted curtains were used at windows until machine netting became available in the nineteenth century. The only tools required for netting are a netting needle and a gauge or mesh the size of the hole you require. Netting boxes are weighted to give them stability and often contain a roller, which is lifted out when in use. Some boxes have thread holders, for different thicknesses of thread, and gauges of varying sizes, either in ivory or metal. The ivory netting needles look like two-pronged forks on which you wind the thread lengthwise.

Meshes or gauges look like slim rulers and they determine the size of the holes. There may be a steel clamp in the box, with a hook at the top to secure the end of the thread. This is clamped to your weighted box to give you a firm start. Nets were made by men for hunting and fishing, as well as by women. You can find most attractive netting sets, with ivory tools contained in carved tortoiseshell cylindrical cases, made in Canton for the export market.

Tatting

Done on a smaller shuttle, tatting involves making a loop and then smaller loops like petals around a flower center. These edgings look a little like lace, and are used to finish linen handkerchiefs, pillow-cases, and general domestic articles. It is comparatively easy to do. The American shuttles often have a hook, or one sharp end, which enables you to attach each of the loops without recourse to another tool. In tatting sets, you may find a hook on a chain, suspended from a finger ring. Alternatively, a crochet hook can be used.

Tambour Work

Tambour work is done on a round wooden frame in the shape of a drum, hence the name *tambour*, which is French for drum. The work is done from the underside with a running thread and requires the use of a spool knave. The spool knave looks like a stirrup and holds the thread, enabling it to run evenly and continuously. The knave is usually suspended from the waist by means of a waist hook. The stitch is mainly chain-stitch, which is done by making a loop and then pulling the thread through with a hook. The cover of the hook unscrews to reveal a metal hook. This can then be screwed onto the base of the hook handle in order not to lose it. Today, people who are not used to seeing the cover attached to the other end imagine that the top is missing— this may allow those more knowledgeable to buy one cheaply.

Cord Making

Cords were used for many purposes, from threading through clothes to making draw-strings for purses. Bigger cords were used for finishing upholstery and tying back curtains. The thickness of the thread determined the diameter of the cord. All you needed was a lucet, a kind of two-pronged fork. The technique involved winding the thread or silk around the two prongs. Then, by lifting the lower thread over the prong and forming a figure eight, you made a cord that resembled plaiting. Lucets can be found in ivory, bone, mother-of-pearl, and wood with some versions having a handle.

Drizzling or Parsiflage

Drizzling was really just unpicking, mainly of gold and silver thread, in order to re-use it. In a drizzling set there are two unpicking tools, a knife and a stiletto, on either side of a pair of scissors, which were for cutting the thread. The sets were often made in silver or enamel, and suspended on a chain. Sometimes you find a boxed set, in which there is a small spinning device for spinning and storing the thread.

Appendix II

Glossary of Sewing Tools

This glossary lists sewing tools and related terms in alphabetical order to help with identification and understanding of their purpose.

Avery & Son, of Redditch, were famous for making needle packet containers in decorative brass, often in novelty shapes such as wheelbarrows and butterflies. Main period 1868 to end of the nineteenth century.

Bodkin looks like a large needle but has a blunt end and large eye for threading ribbon, tape, and thick thread through holes. Can be made from many different materials; used since the earliest days of sewing to today. Often found in étuis and boxed sewing sets.

Baxter print needle boxes are little cardboard boxes used to hold needle packets (1-2"/2.6-5.2 cm), often in sets of ten. The lids are often decorated with pictures of flowers or scenes. Made from c. 1850-1867.

Blond, of Le Blond & Co., produced very similar color printed boxes to Baxter, but only two designs are recorded.

Bobbins were made mainly in bone or wood and used on lace pillows to make lace during the eighteenth to the nineteenth century.

Châtelaine was a collection of small tools, worn suspended by a clip from a belt around the waist. Made in many different materials through the ages, they often held sewing tools or keys, watches, manicure articles, or anything else considered useful.

Clamps were made in many different materials: wood, ivory, and metal, c. 1790-1880. Fabric would be held in the vice, which was clamped to the table edge and secured by a screw underneath, thus leaving both hands free to cut, pin, or sew.

Crochet hooks are long and thin with a hook at one end; they can be made from ivory, bone, metal, or wood, and the hook is sometimes protected by a guard or case. Can be found in sets of different sized hooks. A form of crochet has existed for many century in many cultures.

Cotton barrels, or cotton reel holders, are most often found in sets in boxes from the nineteenth century. Made in bone, ivory, vegetable ivory, and mother-of-pearl, and used to hold thread before commercial reels.

Darners for gloves have a rounded knob on either end, sometimes of different sizes. Larger darners were mainly for stockings. They were made in many different materials, including glass, throughout the nineteenth and early twentieth centuries.

Ear spoons were used to clean the ears and are often found in sets and boxes from the eighteenth and early nineteenth centuries. They can be found on the end of a bodkin, especially the larger seventeenth century versions.

Emery was a little cushion stuffed with grains of emery, used to remove the rust from needles and pins. It is distinguished from a pin cushion by its heavier weight and compact contents.

Equipage is a French word meaning equipment, and can be used to cover any small set of tools from sewing to picnic to surgical.

Étui is a French word, much used in the eighteenth and nineteenth centuries, which describes a small portable sewing or manicure set.

Girdle spinning wheel is a small spinning wheel which could be tucked into a belt or girdle.

Hemming Bird was a type of gilded brass clamp made in the shape of a bird in the mid-nineteenth century; fish and animals were also popular. Some have pin cushions on top, and the date (Patented Feb 15th 1853) was impressed on the wing.

Knitting needle end guards, or protectors, were made in various materials during the middle of the nineteenth century. They go over the ends of knitting needles and are joined by elastic, cord, or a chain. They were made in novelty shapes.

Knitting sheath is worn tucked into the belt on the right hip, the knitting needle protruding from the hole at the end. Mainly made in wood, but some in ivory or metal, during the eighteenth and nineteenth centuries.

Knotting shuttles were larger than tatting shuttles, and had open ends. They were made in many precious materials, often richly inlaid, and considered an aristocratic tool. Mainly used in the eighteenth century.

Lace pricker, used to unpick lace and often mistaken for a stiletto, is a needle inserted into a handle, sometimes covered by a case. Mainly nineteenth century, made in different materials such as ivory and silver.

Ladies Companion was a case, usually made in an upright form, sometimes in tooled leather disguised as a book, which contained tools, such as thimbles, tape-measures, notebooks, pencils, scent bottles etc. Mainly nineteenth century.

Lucet is a two-pronged fork, sometimes with a handle, made in various materials, such as wood, bone, and silver. It was used to wind thread around to make cords. Mainly eighteenth and nineteenth century.

Nanny brooches were brooches containing emergency sewing sets. The end unscrews to reveal thread around a needle case. Goldstone and various stones were used. The design was patented in 1895.

Needles are the most important tool for sewing, and are as old as time. They were found in gold and silver in Pre-dynastic Egyptian tombs, and are used virtually unchanged today.

Needle cases are for holding needles and are found in virtually every conceivable material, from every period. Most sets and sewing boxes contain a needle holder, needle-book, or needle-box.

Navette is the French word for a shuttle, usually applied to the big knotting variety. It derives from the fact that shuttles are boat-shaped.

Netting sets are sometimes contained in boxes, with hooks, gauges, and clamps, or could be ivory sets in carved tubes, containing various gauges for the net. The two prongs at the end of a stick are to wind the thread around, lengthwise. Mainly late eighteenth to mid-nineteenth century.

Palais Royal is a generic name given to very finely made items, made in Paris in the late eighteenth and early nineteenth centuries, a typical tool being made from mother-of-pearl mounted in gold, with an enamel plaque.

Peeps, also known as Stanhopes, were tiny prints or early photos of popular views, set in a magnifying lens. Peeps were inserted as souvenirs at the end of sewing tools and other keepsakes. Mid-nineteenth century.

Pin-ball was a ball for keeping pins in, often in fine knitting and suspended on a ribbon or chain, and embroidered with a message or date. Some have silver mounts. They predate pin cushions. Mainly seventeenth and early eighteenth century.

Pin cushion is a pad into which pins are pushed for safe keeping. They come in all sorts of materials, shapes, and sizes. Styles have changed through the centuries, but they can always be found in sewing sets and boxes.

Pin-poppet is another earlier version of a pin cushion, but the little cushion is held in a container, often with a top or lid, which unscrews to reveal the pins.

Pin wheel consists of two flat discs with padding between them, into which pins are stuck.

Pricker is another word for a stiletto or awl, a small sharp tool made in various materials such as metal or ivory,

often with a cover to protect the point. It is used to unpick or to make holes for embroidery.

Reel holder can be large or small, in wood or a metal such as brass. They were often very ornate and were made to hold or cover cotton reels in a decorative manner. Mid-nineteenth century.

Sampler was a piece of cloth displaying a variety of stitches, sometimes in an alphabet strip or depicting a scene, with the name of the maker and date of creation. They were executed as an example of skill and can be found—often in sewing boxes—in varying sizes from tiny to picture size.

Scissors are a vital cutting tool used since early history. Made in metal, often with decorative handles. Scissors cases are also very decorative in themselves.

Spool knave is shaped rather like a stirrup, with a horizontal bar which unscrews to take the ball of thread or wool for the task. They were mostly made in metal, or wood and metal, with a clip for attaching to a waist belt. Used in the eighteenth and nineteenth centuries.

Stanhopes see Peeps.

Stiletto is another word for pricker or awl, and is used to unpick or make holes in fabric, for example in *Broderie Anglaise*. Nearly every étui, or sewing set, contains a stiletto.

Swift is a large winder for wool or thread, clamped to a table and opening out like an umbrella.

Tambour hook is similar to a crochet hook, but with a very fine sharp end. Sometimes extra hooks can be contained inside the main shaft. Handles come in many materials: gold, tortoiseshell, and ivory.

Tatting shuttle is smaller than the knotting shuttle, and usually not so ornate. The ends got closer towards the end of the nineteenth century. The shuttles sometimes came with a hook and thread in a case, or box.

Thimbles are shields worn to protect the finger while sewing. Thimbles have been made in every material, and certainly date from the twelfth century until today. Most sewing sets have one, and sometimes a nail-guard as well.

Vinaigrette is a little box which unscrews to reveal a grille, under which was placed vinegar or scent on a sponge or wax. This was used to ward off bad smells or infection. Vinaigrettes are often found in old sewing boxes.

Waxers were often tiny wheels, or two tiny discs with a central post, on which was secured wax. The wax was used on cotton thread to stiffen it so that it could thread more easily through the eye of a needle, or to smooth thread for fine sewing.

Winders were made for winding thread around before reels were invented. They came in a great variety of designs and materials, in flat shapes with points to wind the thread around. Snowflake shapes in mother-of-pearl are often found in old sewing sets and boxes.

Appendix III

A useful nineteenth century chronology of historical landmarks, sometimes used as inspiration by the designers of sewing tools, especially commemorative items. For advice in composing this chronology, I am indebted to the Open University's Victorian Studies section.

1814	George Stephenson constructs the first steam locomotive
1817	*Scotsman* founded
1818	British take over Poona and Indore in India
	First steamship crossing of the Atlantic (26 days)
1819	H.C. Oerstead discovers electromagnetism
1820	First iron steamship
	"Missouri Compromise" limits slavery in the USA
1822	Streets of Boston, Massachusetts lit by gas
1825	Stockton-Darlington railway opens
1826	First railway tunnel (Liverpool-Manchester railway)
1827	Joseph Niepce produces photographs on a metal plate
1830	Liverpool-Manchester railway opens
	July Revolution in Paris brings Louis-Philippe to the throne
1831	Faraday discovers electromagnetic induction
1832	Morse invents the telegraph
	First railway in Europe (Budweis-Linz)
1833	British Factory Act forbids employment of children under nine
1834	Poor Law Amendment Act establishes workhouses
	Slavery abolished in British Empire
1836	British colony in South Australia founded
1837	Accession of Queen Victoria
1838	Start of regular transatlantic steamship service
1839	W.H. Fox Talbot produces a photographic negative
	Daguerre invents Daguerrotype
1840	Penny post in Britain
	Remains of Napoleon I brought to Les Invalides, Paris
1846	Railway boom in Britain
1847	First Gold Rush to California
1848	Pre-Raphaelite Brotherhood
	Year of revolutions in Europe
	W.H. Smith starts railway bookstalls
1850	Dicken's magazine *Household Words* starts
1851	Great Exhibition in London

1854	Crimean War breaks out
	News of the World sells over 100,000 copies in one week
1856	Bessemer's process makes cheap steel possible
	First aniline dye ("mauve") prepared by Perkins
1857	Transatlantic cable laid
	Indian mutiny breaks out
	Matrimonial Causes Act establishes divorce courts in England and Wales; men, but not women, can win divorce on grounds of adultery
1859	Monthly publication of *Beeton's Book of Household Management* begins (1859-61)
1860	Abraham Lincoln, opposing further extension of slavery, elected US President
	Garibaldi, after successful military campaign, proclaims Victor Emmanuel, King of Sardinia, "King of Italy"
	Source of Nile discovered
1861	Prince Albert dies
	American Civil War breaks out
	Railways beginning to expand in Russia: nearly 700 million rubles of private capital invested in 1860s, plus vast government loans
1862	Lincoln declares all US slaves to be free
1863	Football Association founded
1864	Co-operative Wholesale Society starts
1865	American Civil War ends
	Assassination of Lincoln
	First "bone-shaker" bicycle
	First carpet sweeper
	First mechanical dishwasher
	Atlantic Cable finally successful
	Joseph Lister initiates antiseptic surgery
1867	Canada becomes a dominion
	Paris World Fair introduces Japanese Art to the West
1868	Abolition in Britain of public execution
1869	Opening of the Suez Canal
	State of Wyoming enfranchises women
	Invention of margarine and celluloid
	First electric washing-machine
	Sophia Jex Blake admitted to classes in medicine at Edinburgh University

1870	Franco-Prussian War
	Napoleon III deposed: French republic
	Irish Home Rule movement launched
1871	Bank holidays introduced in England and Wales
	First women students' residence in Cambridge
1872	First F.A. Cup
	Railways expanding fast in Russia: freight carried more than quadruples in 1870s
1873	Remington typewriter produced
	First Girls' Public Day School
1874	Lawn tennis invented
	Medical school for women in London
	First 'Impressionist' exhibition in Paris (Monet, Renoir, Cezanne, Degas, etc.)
1876	Queen Victoria declared Empress of India
	A.G. Bell invents telephone
	Edison invents phonograph
1877	First public telephone
1878	Microphone invented
	Earliest electric street lighting in London
	Bicycle Touring Club founded in England
	London University opens degrees to women

1880	School attendance made compulsory in Britain for children aged 5-10
	First Anglo-Boer War: British defeat at Majuba Hill
1882	Married Women's Property Act in Britain gives married women right of separate ownership of property of all kinds
1884	Scramble for Africa—Berlin Conference of fourteen European nations on African affairs
1886	Liberal Government in Britain defeated over Irish Home Rule
1887	Queen Victoria's Golden Jubilee
1888	Kodak box camera invented
1890	First elementary education in Britain
	First underground railway in London
1893	Women get the vote in New Zealand
1897	Queen Victoria's Diamond Jubilee celebrated
	C.R. Macintosh's Glasgow School of Art pioneers "modernist" Art Nouveau architecture
1901	Queen Victoria dies
	First motor-bicycle

Endnotes

Introduction
[1] Information supplied by the British Museum.

Chapter One
[1] Barbara A. Hanawalt, editor, *Women and Work in Preindustrial Europe* (Indiana: Indiana University Press, 1986).
[2] Henry Mayhew, *London Labour and the London Poor*, 1851.
[3] Museum of London, Medieval section.

Chapter Two
[1] Olwen Hufton, *The Prospect Before Her, Volume One 1500-1800* (London: Harper Collins, 1995).
[2] Edwin F. Holmes, *A History of Thimbles*.
[3] Charles Oman, *English Engraved Silver, 1150-1900* (London: Faber & Faber, 1978).

Chapter Three
[1] Pamela Clabburn, *The National Trust Book of Furnishing Textiles*.
[2] Christine and David Springett, *Success of the Lace Pillow* (Rugby: C & D Springett, 1997).
[3] Ada Longfield, *Irish Lace* (Dublin: Eason & Son, 1978).

Chapter Four
[1] S. Benjamin, *English Enamel Boxes* (London: Macdonald Orbis, 1978).
[2] Olwen Hufton, *The Prospect Before Her* (London: Harper Collins, 1995).

[3] Information and photos supplied by Molly Pearce, of The Sheffield City Museum, Sheffield.
[4] Information provided by the Sheffield City Museum.
[5] Information from Sotheby's *Objet de Vertu* department.
[6] Nerylla Taunton, *Antique Needlework Tools and Embroideries* (Suffolk: Antique Collectors Club, 1997).
[7] Bridget McConnel, *The Story of the Thimble* (Atglen, Pennsylvania: Schiffer Publishing, Ltd., 1997).
[8] Museum of London, information on London trades in the eighteenth and nineteenth centuries.

Chapter Five
[1] Nerylla Taunton, *Antique Needlework Tools and Embroideries* (Suffolk: Antique Collectors Club, 1997).
[2] "Châtelaines," *Thimble Society Magazine* (1982).
[3] The Mauchlinware Collectors Club can be contacted at Unit 37, Romsey Industrial Estate, Greatbridge Road, Romsey Hampshire, 50510HR, U.K.

Chapter Six
[1] Elizabeth and Douglas Arbittier, and Janet and John Morphy, *Collecting Figural Tapes Measures* (Atglen, Pennsylvania: Schiffer Publishing, Ltd., 1995).
[2] Gay-Ann Rogers, *American Silver Thimbles* (London: Haggerston Press, 1989).

Bibliography

Arbittier, Elizabeth and Douglas, and Janet and John Morphy. *Collecting Figural Tape Measures.* Atglen, Pennsylvania: Schiffer Publishing, Ltd., 1995.

Benjamin, S. *English Enamel Boxes.* London: Macdonald Orbis, 1978.

Clabburn, Pamela. *Furnishing Textiles.* London: Penguin, 1989.

Cummins, G., and N. D. Taunton. *Chatelaines, Utilities to Glorious Extravagance.* Suffolk: Antique Collectors Club, 1996.

Delieb, E. *Investing in Silver.* London: Barnes & Rockliff, 1967.

Groves, Sylvia. *The History of Needlework Tools and Accessories.* Newton Abbot: David & Charles, 1966.

Hanawalt, B.A. *Women and Work in Preindustrial Europe.* Indiana: Indiana University Press, 1986,

Harris, Godfrey. *The Fascination of Ivory.* California: The Americas Group, 1991.

Horowitz, E., and R. Mann. *Victorian Brass Needlecases.* California: Needlework Treasures, 1990.

Hufton, O. *The Prospect Before Her.* London: Harper Collins, 1995.

Longfield, A. *Irish Lace.* Dublin: Eason & Son, 1978.

McConnel, Bridget. *A Collector's Guide to Thimbles.* London: Studio Editions Random House, 1990.

McConnel, Bridget. *The Story of the Thimble.* Atglen, Pennsylvania: Schiffer Publishing, Ltd., 1997.

Oman, Charles. *English Engraved Silver 1150-1900.* London: Faber & Faber, 1978.

Phillips, J.M. *American Silver.* London: Max Parrish, 1949

Rainwater, D.T. *American Jewelry Manufacturers.* West Chester, Pennsylvania: Schiffer Publishing, Ltd., 1988.

Rainwater, D.T. *Encyclopaedia of American Silver Manufacturers.* West Chester, Pennsylvania: Schiffer Publishing, Ltd., 1986.

Rogers, Gay-Ann. *American Silver Thimbles.* London: Haggerston Press, 1989.

Rogers, Gay-Ann. *An Illustrated History of Needlework Tools.* London: John Murray, 1983.

Sandon, Henry. *Royal Worcester Porcelain.* London: Barrie & Jenkins, 1973.

Sawdon, Mary. *A History of Victorian Skirt Grips.* Cambridge: Midsummer Books, 1995.

Springett, Christine, and David Springett. *Success to the Lace Pillow.* Rugby: C & D Springett, 1997.

Taunton, Nerylla. *Antique Needlework Tools and Embroideries.* Suffolk: Antique Collectors Club, 1997.

Wayland Barber, E. *Women's Work, The First 20,000 Years.* New York: Norton Paperback, 1994.

Whiting, Gertrude. *Old Time Tools and Toys of Needlework.* New York: Dover, 1971.

Index

For More Information:
Thimble Society
Portobello Studios
101 Portobello Road
London, England W11 2QB
Tel/Fax: 0171 267 5866

Notes